WHO OWNS
THE FAMILY?

WHO OWNS THE FAMILY?

God or the State?

Ray R. Sutton

DOMINION PRESS • FT. WORTH, TEXAS

THOMAS NELSON, INC. • NASHVILLE • CAMDEN • NEW YORK

Co-published by Dominion Press, Ft. Worth, Texas, and Thomas Nelson, Inc., Nashville, Tennessee.

Printed in the United States of America

Unless otherwise noted, all Scripture quotations are from the New King James Version of the Bible, copyrighted 1984 by Thomas Nelson, Inc., Nashville, Tennessee.

Library of Congress Catalog Card Number 86-050795

ISBN 0-930462-16-5

Dedicated To
Mrs. Anna Falconer Woosley
My Grandmother
And
Mrs. Joretta Williams
My Mother
Who first taught me Christ in word and deed!

TABLE OF CONTENTS

Marriage, ordained in paradise, had time and history in view. Because history is movement, it entails birth, maturity and death. Each generation fulfills its destiny, and another resumes the pilgrimage of history, which is man's destiny and privilege. When God instituted marriage in Eden, before any parents existed, He ordained, "Therefore shall a man leave his father and mother, and shall cleave unto his wife: and they shall be one flesh" (Gen. 2:24). The significance of this verse is very great. The past must be honored; honoring parents involves sometimes their support economically, as needed. But a man must *leave* his father and mother and *cleave* unto his wife. He must break with the one institution to create another. The old must be honored, but history must move forward. The old authority is honored at God's very specific commandment (Deut. 5:16), but the honor of the old requires the creation of the new authority. The new husband must establish his own area of dominion in family and calling. The unchanging authority is not of this world: it is the sovereign and triune God and His revealed and infallible word. Man belongs to time and to history, and, as long as he is in time, he must remain in history. It is the perversity of sin which makes men denounce heaven and eternity, and then work to negate time and history by trying to convert it into heaven. The result is hell on earth.

R. J. Rushdoony*

*Rushdoony, *The Biblical Philosophy of History* (Phillipsburg, NJ: The Presbyterian and Reformed Publishing Company [1969] 1979), p. 61.

EDITOR'S INTRODUCTION
by Gary North

> And do not fear those who kill the body but cannot kill the soul.
> But rather fear Him who is able to destroy both soul and body in
> hell (Matthew 10:28).

God has established three institutional monopolies: family, church, and state. Each of these is a God-ordained government. Each of these is a covenant. There are only three institutional covenant governments. A covenant is always marked by an oath, either explicit (church, family) or sometimes implicit (state citizenship) and sometimes explicit (state law court). Each of these three governments is to protect the other, and each deserves protection from the other.

The oath is central to any covenant. It involves *calling down the wrath of God on the oath-takers*, in time and in eternity, for any violation of the terms of the oath. When the people's fear of God's judgement when violating the terms of the oath declines, the power of the covenant institution also declines.

In the twentieth century, the premier institution in the minds of most people is the state, or civil government. We live in the era of the power religion. The power religion teaches that might makes right, and therefore might *is* right. The logical goal, obviously, is to seek power. If anyone chooses not to seek power, then he becomes tempted by the other great religion of the day, the escape religion. That person seeks to get away from those who use power.

There is a third religion: Biblical dominion religion. It seeks God's comprehensive kingdom, a visible as well as invisible

ix

kingdom that is governed by God's revealed law. Its supporters
act in the confidence that all other things of value will be added
unto those who seek to establish God's kingdom (Matthew 6:33).
This third religion is at last experiencing a revival. It has slept for
over 300 years. It is a threat—no, it is *the* threat—to the power
religionists.

Weakened Covenants

Sadly, the institutional church is simply not taken seriously
these days, either by the humanists or the average church member. The church's covenant-based threat of excommunication
doesn't scare many members, especially Protestants. Churches
refuse to honor each other's excommunications, and as a result,
they have stripped their own authority to just about zero. Now
that they find themselves increasingly under siege by the local tax-
man, the educational bureaucrat, and even the prosecuting attorney (for example, the Oklahoma case of a church successfully
sued by a self-acknowledged adulteress because the church excommunicated her), they have begun to discover the price of historic impotence.

Church officers no longer believe that they, as ordained
Church officers, possess the God-given power and responsibility
before God provisionally to cast men into hell, unless these condemned people publicly repent. They no longer believe Christ's
words to church officers: "Assuredly, I say to you, whatever you
bind on earth will be bound in heaven, and whatever you loose on
earth will be loosed in heaven" (Matthew 18:18). Having lost faith
in their power provisionally to condemn men's eternal souls, they
have also lost faith in the institutional authority of the church. But
if church officers have lost faith in this crucial power of the
church, what protection can they expect today from the self-
imposed fear of pagans?

This leaves the family as the covenant institution that people
think is able to defend itself from the unlawful encroachments of

state power. But family authority is also under siege. Like the loss in authority that the church has suffered, the loss in family authority has come as a result of the very members of the family having abandoned their fear of God, under whom the marriage oath was taken. Divorce rates have soared—a public announcement of people's lack of covenantal fear in God. Family members no longer believe that a vow taken before God has any permanent meaning, let alone any threat of judgment. The oath taken before God has lost its power outside of the civil government's courtroom, where perjury is still a punishable offense—punishable by the state, though not by God, men assume. Men now fear only those who can kill the body.

Thus, the loss of faith in the God who enforces all three covenant oaths *in history* has led to the monopoly of state power in history. The state can kill the body, or at least sentence the body to prison. Since men no longer believe in the earthly or eternal validity of any institutional manifestation of God's power to destroy both body and soul in hell, the oaths of both church and family are regarded either as irrelevant or relevant only when backed up by state power. The state covenant is the only covenant that anyone pays much attention to today.

The church has slid down the slope into cultural impotence. The family is close behind. Only the state remains as a force to be taken seriously in history—and history increasingly is the only thing anyone takes seriously.

A Shift in Opinion

In the last two decades, there has been the beginning of a change in opinion. Christians and non-Christians alike have begun to recognize the historical threat of a collapsing family structure. They have begun to see what Stalin saw in 1936, when he pragmatically imposed rigorous civil laws that protected the Russian family against the acids of original Marxist theories that favored free love and the abolition of the family. He saw that Marxism's theories of the family would destroy the Soviet Union, so the new laws made divorce difficult, abortion illegal, and homosexuality a one-way ticket to the Gulag Archipelago.

Only after 1964 did the Soviets reverse this Stalinist pro-family heritage, at exactly the same time that the humanist assault on the family began in earnest in the West. All over the West in 1965, pro-abortion literature began to pour off the presses. The Rockefeller and Ford Foundations spend over $246 million, 1965-76, to promote family planning propaganda.[1]

Simultaneously in the United States, the independent Christian school movement went into high gear (well, second gear, anyway). A growing number of Christians at last realized the truth of what church historian Sidney Mead has said, "the public-school system of the United States *is* its established church."[2] They finally decided to pull their children out of the humanists' established church, a church coercively financed at the expense of 60 million Christians.

The astounding success of the pro-family ministry of James Dobson (author of the best-selling book, *Dare to Discipline*) — he receives 150,000 letters *per month* — and the media-ignored success of Bill Gothard's sports arena-filling but unadvertised seminars, "Basic Youth Concepts," indicate that Christians have begun to restore their confidence in the family as a covenant institution. The possibility of a breakdown in the family is not just a danger close to home; it is a danger *to* the home. A collapse here cannot be ignored, the way a collapse of church authority can be ignored (for a while).

A Declaration of War

What a growing number of Christians have begun to understand since 1980 is that their renewed support of the family necessarily involves them in a war against the state. The state has encroached steadily on family authority for over a century, and fear-

1. Julian Simon, *The Ultimate Resource* (Princeton: Princeton University Press, 1981), p. 292.

2. Sidney E. Mead, *The Lively Experiment: The Shaping of Christianity in America* (New York: Harper & Row, 1963), p. 68.

fully since 1965. Thus, what may initially appear to be merely a defense of the integrity of the family *necessarily* leads to an offense against unlawful state power. It is the war between two irreconcilable religions, the religion of the Bible and the religion of state-deifying secular humanism. There can be no permanent peace treaty between the two camps. There will be winners and losers, on earth and in eternity.

The humanists are going to be the losers, not simply in eternity but also in history. Fearful retreatist Christians refuse to believe this, so they stay on the sidelines of life, as they have stayed for over a century. They will continue to cry out to the forces of the dominion religion to pull back, to cut another unworkable deal with the humanists, and to content ourselves with a cease-fire. Cease-fires with Satan don't last, either with the public schools or the Soviet Union. There is a war to the death going on.

This book is a call to Christians to join the winning side.

INTRODUCTION

The family in America is under *siege*.
I know it.
You know it.
We all feel the truth of the words of a social scientist, "People are scared. They see relationships collapsing all around them, and they worry about whether theirs will last. But they don't know what to do about it."

But when I say the family is under siege, I mean an all-out war is being waged against it!

The statistics in so many areas that touch the family are alarming.

> The divorce rate has more than doubled since 1971. A staggering 1.2 million divorces in 1985 affected 1.8 million children.
>
> Single-parent families are growing at 20 times the rate of two-parent families.
>
> More frightening is the expanding number of one-parent families with children who live with a mother *who has never been married*. Since 1970, there has been a four-fold increase (2.8 million) in the children being reared by a mother who has never been married.

But even though the family is under siege, most do not know where the attack is coming from.

Attack From Outside

Do you know where the attack is coming from?

Rarely do students of human behavior agree on anything, but an article in the August 1974 issue of *Scientific American*, "The Origins of Alienation," said there are two "generalizations" being agreed upon about research on our society.

(1) Social disorder in our culture results from complete *family disorganization*, and

(2) "Much of the same research also shows that the forces of disorganization arise primarily not from within the family but from the *circumstances in which the family finds itself* and *from the way of life that is imposed on it by those circumstances.*"

Exactly!

I know of so many parents who are trying to raise a family, but they feel like they're *swimming upstream*.

It seems like everything and almost everyone in our society is against the family—the very thing most dear to them.

There may be those who "pretend" to defend the family, but time after time, we find that their solutions are just as much a part of the problem as the solutions recommended by someone who comes right out and attacks the family.

It's like an interview in the March 15, 1979 issue of the *Dallas Morning News* with Betty Friedan, founder of the National Organization for Women, and with the "mother of Women's Lib," Muriel Fox.

They seemed to care about the family, admitting that it is in "a hopeless state of collapse." Their proposal: "Innovative and practical solutions."

What do they mean?

Their definition of the family says it all: "Family is people who are living together with deep commitment and with mutual needs and sharing."

Get the point?

A family is *anybody*, even lesbians and homosexuals, "living together with deep commitment."

It doesn't make any difference whether a family is built on a *heterosexual* relationship. What really counts is the commitment, even if it is perverted!

So, just because people say they are "for the family" doesn't necessarily mean anything. They may be, and probably are, part of the unloyal opposition against the traditional household.

But let's get specific. "Who" or "what" are these "forces of disorganization" waging war? Who's the real enemy out there?

Public Enemy #1

Perhaps you've heard the slogan, "With friends like you, who needs enemies?" I can't list all the "enemies of the family," but I can isolate public enemy #1: *today's civil government.*

That's right.

Over the last 50 years, the social and economic policies of the civil government, as well as its legislation against the family, have dealt one death blow after another. It's not supposed to be this way. God created the civil government to protect the society of which family is such an important part. But it's just not this way right now in our society. In fact, every time the government says it's going to do something to help the family, watch out!

Remember the Carter Administration? In 1979, President Carter decided to try to "help" the family, since it was being strained to the breaking point by social and economic forces "beyond its control." His aid was in the form of the creation of the "Office For Families," part of the Department of Health, Education, and Welfare (HEW). One author said this was "kind of like putting goats in charge of the cabbage patch."

First on the "list of things to do" were three conferences, beginning in 1980, to determine whether government, private enterprise, and business were helping or hurting the family.

How well I remember the Baltimore session of the White House Conference on the family. One delegate immediately asked the conference to define the family as "two or more persons who share resources, responsibility for decisions, values and goals, and have commitment to one another over time." Sounds similar to what Ms. Friedan and Fox tried to do.

The really horrifying scene was that the action lost only by two votes out of 761 delegates!

The whole conference went on this way, providing a forum for liberals to re-define the family.

It would have gone the same way in Virginia's session, except that a dedicated pro-family lady named Jo Ann Gasper saw what was coming and organized a counter-move at the last minute. The Virginia convention was well attended by pro-family women who didn't pass anti-family resolutions. But if she hadn't been alerted to the potential misuse of this forum by anti-family forces, it would have been a disaster. As the organizer of the anti-family delegates later admitted to her, "You wiped out a year of my life." (Mrs. Gasper later was appointed by the Reagan Administration to a high-level position in the Department of Health and Human Services.)

So, the "good friend" of the family, Jimmy Carter, tried to take governmental action to support the modern household, but it turned out to be disastrous.

Every time the civil government tries to form social and economic programs to help, these very programs create what they are "supposedly" trying to remove. Why should this be?

The answer is simple: the State buys problems.

Failure of Government Programs

Years ago, local governments would set up money bounties for troublesome rodents or animals that the public wanted to eliminate. It would pay money if someone would bring in proof of having exterminated a pest, such as a rat's tail or a pair of ears from a coyote.

Guess what happened? If the bounties were high enough to affect people's plans, eventually some enterprising people would start breeding rats or coyotes for a living. They would take in piles of tails or ears and collect their reward. After all, it's a lot easier to breed rats in a shed or barn than catch them. The result of the bounties was the opposite of what was officially intended. The community would wind up with more of the unwanted pests than before the program began.

Paying People Not to Be Self-Reliant

This is exactly what happens when the civil government tries to create welfare programs. Like the rat-tail bounty, welfare programs actually create what they are trying to remove. The costs of the programs go higher and higher.

When the government pays money to people who are unable to support themselves, it creates an incentive to become non-supporting. People who were just getting by—barely self-reliant people—now see an opportunity. They can register as *officially non-self-reliant people* and collect easy money. It pays the marginally productive to "go over the line" into official poverty. It pulls them out of the free market (where there is always at least the hope of increasing one's responsibility and income) and into the welfare world, where there is very little hope of escaping the cycle of poverty.

Charles Murray's whole point in his detailed book *Losing Ground* (1984) is that the "welfare and poverty" programs of the early 60s have increased poverty, crime, and welfare among the minorities. Quite a startling statement from a man who is a political liberal in many of his views!

We might say that the free market responds to monetary demand, no matter what that demand is for. If there is new government demand for poverty victims, then the market will respond and produce such victims in greater abundance than before the program was begun.

The Family

When it comes to the family, there's no difference. We see the same process.

The government's economic policies have antagonized the family. The government has become family enemy #1.

Notice in the chart below that the years from 1960-1980 produced extremely high rates of *illegitimate births*. In 1960, approximately 224,000 children were born to single mothers. But in 1980, the number jumped to 665,747.

Why?

Murray points out that it was during this same period of history that all the schemes of the Great Society appeared. The more the government pumped into welfare, the more illegitimacy rose.

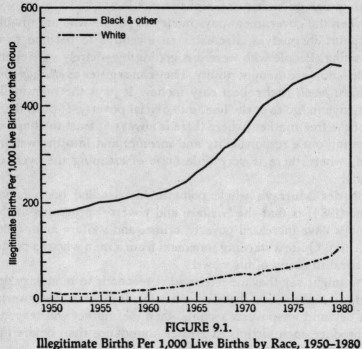

FIGURE 9.1.
Illegitimate Births Per 1,000 Live Births by Race, 1950–1980
DATA AND SOURCE INFORMATION: Appendix table 24.

It's simple. The government can't legislate social welfare. Pick an area, any area, and you'll discover that government involvement in social issues has become disasterous. The statistics on illegitimacy are obvious. Are there any others?

Adoption Problems Created by the Government

Today in the United States, about 1.5 million infants are killed each year in the womb. The world-wide total has been estimated by government agencies to be as high as 35 million a year.

Today, it also is difficult to *adopt*. It's not that many people don't want to adopt children, but there are numerous *adoption barriers*, most of which are created by the government, and they feed back into the abortion problem.

How so?

The government places "price ceilings" on adoption fees and

maternity care expenses that are so low that they don't actually cover expenses. Supposedly, the government wants to prevent "baby-buying" and sets ceilings, for example, in the District of Columbia, at $2,500. This means that the adoption agency cannot pay for the maternity home care. This closes off a potential solution for the pregnant girl. She often finds it easier, and less expensive, to have her own child destroyed in an abortion chamber (Abortion Clinic).

Here is a classic example where a "free-market" approach to unwanted pregnancies would "pay" mothers to carry their children full-term and allow them to be adopted.

Let's get our terminology clear. The Bible is clear: kidnapping carries the death penalty (Exodus 21:16). The Bible teaches that a society that honors God must inflict the highest possible penalty on kidnapping in order to discourage the practice. Because of this ever-present threat, it is legitimate for civil government to require adoption agencies to keep careful records about the source of supply for any child, and to limit legal adoptions to transactions with these conforming agencies.

Second, the Bible is clear that promiscuity is evil. It should be restricted by government, but not *civil* government. It should be restricted by *church* and *family* governments. The Church has a legitimate concern for morality among its members. If the parents fail to discipline their children, then the Church should get involved in some sort of discipline (Matthew 18:15-18).

But family government is supposed to be the main parameter for promiscuity. The head of the household of the daughter who becomes pregnant is to decide whether to compel the marriage between the sinning daughter and her sinning male consort. If the parent decides against the marriage, he or she can demand that the male (or his family) pay a sufficient amount of money to pay for the birth of the baby—not its execution, but its birth. The civil government does not have any independent authority in this regard; it simply supports the decision of the legally sovereign parent (Deuteronomy 22:28-29).

Finally, if the unmarried daughter decides to have an adopting family pay for the expenses, she can keep the money paid by her consort—what in some societies might be called a dowry. It gives her some protective capital before she enters a marriage—something that is hers that she takes into the marriage. (By the way, American fathers of the bride pay for expensive weddings, and guests bring lots of gifts. If this isn't a dowry, it's only because the gifts wear out; in dowry societies, the father gives the bride silver or other assets, and this is her property for life—protection in case she is divorced by her husband.)

Any attempt to label such an adoption fee transaction a free market "baby for sale" operation misses the point. The idea is, first, to place financial incentives on saving the life of the child (through adoption expenses), and second, to reduce the incentive for illicit fornication (through parental authority over the unmarried couple).

But civil government interferes with the first and will not back up the second, and it therefore becomes a main opponent of the family. In fact, the National Adoption Exchange complains that in some areas of the country relatives are not allowed to adopt a child because of a rigid "age 40" limit.

This anti-adoption policy indirectly subsidizes the abortion clinics. The government needs to get out of the subsidy business. Indeed, in almost every case, low-income homes with loving parents would be much better than a "tax-subsidized," lower-qualified, government-approved foster home.

Government on Divorce

In 1981, Nye and McDonald did a study where they asked the major leadership groups, "Should divorce in this country be easier or more difficult to obtain than it is now?" The results are described below.

Take a look at the two groups that had the weakest response in the "more difficult" category: Government and Law & Justice.

This means we have a tremendous *value gap* between the populace and government. This means the government is pro-family as it approaches election day, but pro-divorce any other time.

LEADERSHIP GROUPS ON DIVORCE

"Should Divorce in This Country Be Easier or More Difficult to Obtain Than It Is Now?"

	MORE DIFFICULT	REMAIN THE SAME	EASIER	TOTAL
Religious	59%	34%	7%	100%
General Public	52%	27%	27%	100%
Business	27%	55%	18%	100%
News Media	27%	51%	22%	100%
Government	21%	53%	26%	100%
Law & Justice	19%	53%	28%	100%

This means the government is privately and publicly at war with the family.

This reminds me of an astounding case I heard about. Although it didn't take place in America, it certainly represented the same kind of practice in this country. In *The London Times*, May 20, 1978, it was reported that a divorce was granted to the wife of a man who *whistled and sang.*

> Mr. Walter Judge, aged sixty-seven, carried his habit of whistling and singing to such extremes that his wife found it intolerable. . . . Mrs. Judge was granted a divorce because the marriage had broken down due to her husband's unreasonable behavior.

The family is under siege. It is being attacked from all sides. The greatest enemy is the government itself. What are we to do? Is there an answer?

Yes!

A Biblical Blueprint for the Family

It seems like everything else has been tried.

How about the Bible? *Our nation used to believe that it was the yardstick by which everything, including the family, was measured.*

How many people still believe this? Don't be surprised. More and more people perceive we've gotten away from our *Biblical foundation*! But they don't know what to do.

Here's where we come to the concern of this book.

No one in his right mind would think of building a house without some sort of blueprint to follow. Yet millions of Americans are trying to build their *families* without consulting *God's blueprint*, the Bible.

Doesn't it make sense that we would be successful if we did it *God's way?*

So, before we can defend ourselves against the enemies of the family, and particularly the economic and legal policies of the civil government, we need to listen to God!

I think we need to ask a very fundamental question: *Who Owns the Family?*

I've discovered that a lot of people don't realize that this is the heart of all the problems concerning the family. If you don't own something, you don't control it. This seems so obvious, doesn't it? But how many times have you discovered the source of a problem was that you just didn't consider the obvious?

It's quite obvious that the civil government knows this is the major question to be answered.

How do I know?

Take a look at all the legislation coming out of the judicial branch of the government. Remember, this is the *law and justice* group that we saw was so weak on the divorce question.

Over the last 50 years the government has been systematically legislating family ownership away from the rightful owner.

If you don't believe me, then you need to read this book. Even if you do believe me, I'll bet you don't know the *10 cases that changed American family life*. You too need to examine the contents of the following pages.

Who Owns the Family is organized into two sections: principles and practical application.

In the *principles* section, I will present 10 principles in answer to the question, "Who owns the family?"

Each chapter centers around a *major court case* that violates or supports one of the ten principles. Since most of the recent court cases concerning the family have attacked it, the majority of the examples I use are negative.

In my opinion, *these are 10 court cases that have established precedents that either have altered or could alter our families' lives*. The point is, I'm not making up these concerns. These concerns are a matter of law.

In the practical application section, I want specifically to tell you how each of the spheres of society — family, church, and state — can put ownership back into the rightful hands.

When we finish, we will know who owns the family, what this means, and how to put the family back on course in our society.

But first, we should understand *who owns the family*. Does the State? Does the Church? How about the parents? Do they own the family?

Let's take a look at the first chapter to find out.

Part I
BLUEPRINTS

1

A COVENANT, NOT A CONTRACT

Who owns the family? The State? The Church? The parents? All of these answers are wrong.

God owns the family!

Any time you try to argue that someone, or some "institution," owns the family, you will end up viewing the family as just a *human* creation, a mere contract. If that's all it is, then there's no reason for the State not to violate it, just as it violates all sorts of private contracts. What principle is to prevent the State from taking a family's children, re-educating them, or breaking it up whenever it seems socially or politically expedient?

Ironically, the State used to be the biggest defender of the family and parental rights over children because the U.S. Supreme Court ruled that *marriage is more than a contract.* Almost 100 years ago, there was an important case, *Maynard v. Hill* (1888), that made this point. The United States Supreme Court said:

> [W]hilst marriage is often termed by text writers and in decisions of courts a civil contract . . . *it is something more than a mere contract.* The consent of the parties is of course essential to its existence, but when the contract to marry is executed by the marriage, a relation between the parties is created which they cannot change. Other contracts may be modified, restricted, or enlarged, or entirely released upon the consent of the parties.
>
> Not so with marriage. The relation once formed, the law steps in and holds the parties to various obligations and liabilities. *It is an institution,* the maintenance of which in its purity the public is deeply interested, for it is the foundation of the family and of society, without which there would be neither civilization nor progress (emphasis mine).

3

I know it's hard to believe that the Supreme Court once said such a thing, but it's true. There is real legal precedent that marriage is not just a contract.

Well, if it's not a contract, then what is it? The language of the Supreme Court is that it is an *institution*. So what? Since marriage is an "institution," it is a *sacred covenant*.

A Sacred Covenant

A few years ago, I was with some friends. After dinner, I happened to notice a faded-out, old document on the table. I couldn't make out the words, but in big bold letters at the top of the document it said, "Marriage Covenant between. . . ."

I couldn't believe my eyes. I asked my friend what this was. He told me it was a marriage covenant, filed at the local courthouse, between his great, great, great grandparents.

An immediate question popped into my head: "When did people stop drawing up marriage covenants?"

The answer to that question turned out to be a fascinating study, one that I can't go into at this point. But it is quite clear that marriages in this country, 100, 200, and even 300 years ago, were viewed as *sacred covenants*. Below, you'll find a covenant dating from 1664/1665. (Two years are listed because in the old days — the 17th century — the shift to the modern calendar hadn't taken place. The new year came in March. So what they called 1664, we call 1665.) Even though it is called a "contract," notice that the wording of the document itself calls it a *covenant*.

Marriage Contract
January 20, 1664/65
Plymouth, Massachusetts

This writing witnesses, between Thomas Clarke, late of Plymouth, yeoman, and Alice Nicholls of Boston, widow, that, whereas there is an intent of marriage between the said parties, the Lord succeeding their intentions in convenient time; the agreement, therefore, is that the housing and land now in the possession of the said Alice Nicholls shall be reserved as a stock for her son, John Nicholls, for him to enjoy and possess at the age of twenty and one years, in the meantime to be improved by the parents towards his education. Also, that what estate of hers the said Alice shall be found and committed to the said Mr. Clarke, if it should so please the Lord to take the said Alice out of this life before the said Thomas Clarke, she shall then have the power to dispose of all the said estate sometimes hers so as it seems good to her. Moreover, if it shall please the Lord to take away the said Thomas Clarke by death before the said Alice, she surviving, then the said Alice shall have and enjoy her own estate she brought with her, or the value thereof, and two hundred pounds added thereto of the estate left by the said Thomas Clarke. All which the said Thomas Clarke does hereby promise and bind himself to allow of and perform as a *covenant* upon their marriage. In witness of all which, the said Thomas Clarke has signed and sealed this present writing to Peter Oliver and William Bartholmew of Boston, for the use and behoof of the said Alice Nicholls. Dated this twentieth day of January 1664.

per me,   Thomas Clarke

Marriage covenants, like this one, used to be standard. Whenever someone got married, the two worked out a covenant. Today, however, it's quite different. Marriage licenses, drawn up by the *State*, are used. What are they for? Some states have debated their meaning, but generally there is precedent that a marriage license is a *health notification*. It is not a statement of *permission*. (There was a time in American history when in certain southern states it did involve permission, when people of two races were involved.)

I don't think there is anything wrong with this, as long as it doesn't become more than a *health notification*. In a day when AIDS is a growing concern, as a matter of fact, I would think that someone would want to make sure he is not marrying a person with this, or some other awful sexual disease. This would then place the civil marriage license under the general civil quarantine provisions of Leviticus 13 and 14.

The problem is not so much with the marriage license, but

with the fact that that's usually all there is. There is no covenant —
no sense that marriage is more than a mere contract.

The reason is simple. When a marriage covenant is drawn up
and filed at the courthouse, it's hard to secure a divorce. Very
hard! So, in a day when our nation has turned away from God,
we should expect that the whole "covenantal" force of marriage is
ignored.

But what is a covenant? If the State has ruled that this is what
made marriage more than just a contract, an "institution," and if it
proves that God owns the family, we should begin by defining a
covenant.

The Biblical Covenant

"Covenant" is a Biblical word, found many times all through
the Scripture. God's Word is even divided into an Old Covenant,
often called Old "Testament," and New Covenant, or New "Testament" (Hebrews 8:7, 13).

A "covenant" is a *Divinely created bond*. The Old Testament's
Book of Deuteronomy gives us a model. How do we know that it's
a covenant? Because it's the second ("deutero") giving of the Ten
Commandments ("nomy"). Of the first copy, Moses says, "So He
declared to you His *covenant* which He commanded you to perform, that is, the ten commandments; and He wrote them on two
tablets of stone" (Deuteronomy 4:13). Since Deuteronomy is the
second giving of the law, it's the second "covenant" with Israel.

Also, at the end of Deuteronomy, Moses calls the whole book
a covenant when he says, "So keep all of the words of this *covenant*
to do them, that you may prosper in all that you do" (Deuteronomy 29:9).

A Five-Part Program

Since Deuteronomy is a covenant, it becomes a guide. A quick
overview will help us to understand its *five* parts.

1. *Transcendence* (Deuteronomy 1:1-3). A Biblical covenant is
established by God, not man. The covenant, therefore, always
begins by pointing to God's *transcendence*. This word means "to rise

above." Biblically, it means that God is *distinct*. God is the Divine author of the covenant.

The first part of the Deuteronomic covenant says, "Moses spoke to the children of Israel according to all that the *Lord had given him as commandments to them*" (Deuteronomy 1:3). This covenant did not come from man; it was not just a convenient arrangement between two equal parties. It was Divinely created; it rose above man; it was more than a mere contract; it was *sacred*.

2. *Hierarchy* (Deuteronomy 1:6-49). The second part of the covenant lays out the relationship between God's *authority structure* (hierarchy) and the progress (history) of His people. Moses begins the section: "So I took the heads of your tribes, wise and knowledgeable men, and made them heads over you, leaders of thousands, leaders of hundreds, leaders of fifties, leaders of tens, and officers for your tribes" (Deuteronomy 1:15). These leaders represented the Lord's authority: *The Word of God*. As long as the leaders and Israel obeyed the Scripture, there was success. Rebellion, however, led to defeat.

3. *Ethics* (Deuteronomy 5-26). The third section is called "ethics," because it summarizes and expands the Ten Commandments. Fulfillment of righteousness (Faithfulness) is the heart of the covenant. The largest section of Deuteronomy, it specifies two classes of people: The covenant-keeper who is rewarded with blessing, and the covenant-breaker who receives cursing.

4. *Sanctions* (Deuteronomy 27-30). "Sanctions" were positive and negative: blessing and cursing. This section described how the covenant was actually created by a sacred vow, an "oath." In the Old Testament, this oath was accompanied by a symbol called *circumcision* (Genesis 17). Here in Deuteronomy, the oath was actually a *renewal* of circumcision by means of a worship service.

This oath, however, was *self-maledictory* ("declaring evil on oneself"). When a person cut a covenant with the Lord, he was pledging himself *unto death*. In other words, if he ever turned away from his covenant, then it was understood that he would forfeit his life. Only God can make this kind of demand. Thus, the only place where such an oath is valid and binding is in a covenant structure under God. If such an oath is not present, explicitly or implicitly, then the structure isn't a covenant.

5. *Continuity* (Deuteronomy 31-34). Finally, the covenant created a special "bond," *continuity.* Anyone who pledged himself through the self-maledictory oath entered into a bond with God and His people. Faithfulness to this bond, by doing what was described in chapters 5-26 (the ethics section), led to *inheritance.* Those who were covenant-keepers were legitimate heirs. Those who were covenant-breakers were illegitimate, and were disinherited, losing *continuity.*

The Biblical covenant is a *Divinely created bond,* consisting of these five parts. What does this have to do with the family? Remember, the State declared that the family is a *sacred covenant,* an "institution."

Let's apply the covenant model to the family.

The Marriage Covenant

Scripture calls marriage a covenant. The prophet Malachi says, "The Lord has been witness between you and the wife of your youth. . . . She is your companion and your wife by *covenant*" (Malachi 2:14). Since marriage is a *covenant,* the creation of the first family has the same five-fold structure.

> And the Lord God said, "It is not good that man should be alone; I will make him a helper comparable to him." Out of the ground the Lord God formed every beast of the field and every bird of the air, and brought them to Adam to see what he would call them. And whatever Adam called each living creature, that was its name.
>
> So Adam gave names to all the cattle, to the birds of the air, and to every beast of the field. But for Adam there was not found a helper comparable to him. And the Lord God caused a deep sleep to fall on Adam, and he slept; and He took one of his ribs, and closed up the flesh in its place. Then the rib which the Lord God had taken from man He made into a woman, and He brought her to the man. And Adam said:

gh time. Discontinuity means a cutting off in the midst of a disruption.

Moses says that Adam and Eve were "naked and not ashamed." expresses a break in their previous *continuity*. How? Moses s us to see that pre-Fall man and woman lived in a perfect d union. Their nakedness was not a source of shame. After fall into sin, however, their nakedness became a source of . Each recognized in himself the looming prospect of death, God's judgment came. This meant the coming dissolution eir marriage: *divorce by death*. Each faced a partner who in iple was no longer a legal marriage partner. *They had become strangers.*

ovenant-keeping leads to continuity, and covenant-breaking to discontinuity. Family continuity is created to be based on fulness to God's covenant. The following chapters of Genesis as a good example. After the Fall of Adam and Eve, we read t the story of Cain and Abel, the first two sons of this marri- Genesis 4). Cain killed Abel. Because of this, he was cut out e family, and driven away (Genesis 4:14). So, if a member of amily rebels against God's Word, he should be cut out of the ance. But if he's faithful, he should receive an *inheritance*.

ave you ever thought about how the civil government has in- red with the Biblical laws of inheritance? For one, since the years of this century, income tax has seriously cut into every- ability to pass down a hefty financial legacy to his heirs. This one of the severest blows dealt to the family.

evertheless, at this point it is worth observing that Biblical nuity is according to the covenant, not "blood lines." If you about it, all families are initially established by covenant . The *legal* is the basis of the *physical*. So, family "ties" should ased on God's covenant. Family covenant-keepers are sup- d to receive the inheritance. Covenant-breakers are not osed to get anything.

hus, the family is a sacred covenant, more than a contract. powerful effect is that God is the author. Not the State. Not Church. Not even the family. Rather, God's family is trustee five-part sacred covenant.

"This is now bone of my bones
And flesh of my flesh;
She shall be called Woman,
Because she was taken out of Man."

Therefore a man shall leave his father and mother and be joined to his wife, and they shall become one flesh. And they were both naked, the man and his wife, and were not ashamed (Genesis 2:18-25).

1. *Transcendence* (Genesis 2:18). The marriage covenant begins, "Then God said." Notice the similarity between this comment and the beginning of Deuteronomy. God's Word establishes the covenant in both cases.

God created the family, making it a "Divine" institution. I don't mean "Divine" in the sense that it becomes God. Rather, it has a Divine origin. In the traditional church wedding ceremony, the minister quotes Jesus and says, "What God has joined together, let not man separate" (Mark 10:9). God forms a marriage union, just as He created the first one.

This is the family's greatest defense against an encroaching State. *God* gave the parents a Divine trusteeship. When the State attacks the family, it makes war with a sacred covenant; it steps onto a battlefield with God.

2. *Hierarchy* (Genesis 2:19-22). Biblical hierarchy has to do with authority. What is the authority of the family? It has been given an assignment of subduing the earth to the glory of God. We sometimes call this the "cultural mandate." Not just the male, but male and female are called to have authority and dominion over the earth. God said, "Let Us make man in Our image, according to Our likeness; let them (male and female) have dominion over the fish of the sea, over the birds of the air, and over the cattle, over all the earth and over every creeping thing that creeps on the earth" (Genesis 1:26).

God shows Adam this hierarchy by giving him the job of naming the animals. Adam learns two things. One, he has authority over all the earth. Two, he cannot fulfill the mandate by himself. He needs a partner.

God brought the "helper" Adam needed. To paraphrase one theologian, "He did not create Eve from Adam's foot that he might crush her. Nor did He make her from his head that she might dominate him. Rather, she was taken from his side that she might rule with him."

But in the creation of "Woman," God made another hierarchical distinction. Although male and female *together* were to have dominion, the male was given a special "functional headship" over the woman. Paul says, "I do not permit a woman to teach or to have authority over a man . . . for Adam was formed first, then Eve" (1 Timothy 2:12-13).

A functional distinction doesn't imply anything about comparative ethics or comparative worth. All it does is to establish the fact that one person in the relationship has a different set of responsibilities from another. Jesus submitted Himself to the Father *functionally*. He did His Father's business. He didn't subordinate Himself in terms of His "being" or His ethics. He was and is equal to the Father in glory and majesty. He just has a different job in history.

So, together men and women are to dominate the earth. But the male was appointed an organizational leader. Like the sign on former President Harry Truman's desk, "The buck stops here," so does the husband have to take final responsibility for his family before God. The woman is the husband's top advisor. The husband cannot legitimately "pass the buck" by blaming his wife. That's just what Adam tried to do in the garden. He said to God, "The woman whom You gave to be with me, she gave me of the tree, and I ate" (Genesis 3:12). She, in turn, blamed Satan. She was supposed to be under her husband's authority and over Satan with him; they got it backwards in their sin. Satan wound up the victor. The buck nevertheless stopped with each of them, in God's own time. But He demonstrated which place each of them was supposed to have when He cross-examined each of them in turn: Adam, Eve, and Satan.

3. *Ethics* (Genesis 2:23). "Ethics" is the law system of the covenant. In this verse, however, Adam *names* the female. What does

"naming" have to do with God's law? God "c[...] ion over the animals, and then brought some [...] This "classification" of them was the dominio[...] given to Adam. So, when Adam "names" the [...] out God's law. God's law governs the first fam[...]

Freedom is the God-given liberty to *obey*, [...] disobeying God. The family's greatest argume[...] onistic civil government is that it asserts its G[...] to *obey* God's law. *When the civil government will n[...] children according to God's law, then it is making [...]* This is the argument God blesses; this was t[...] forefathers' coming to this continent. They beli[...] of the family covenant is the Word of God.

4. *Sanctions* (Genesis 2:24). The Biblical [...] by an "oath," the ceremonial reception of san[...] riage. As the traditional marriage vows indi[...] oath is "self-maledictory": "Till death us do pa[...] *pledge*. It is binding until the death of a partner. [...] pledge implies death to the one who does n[...] marriage until the death of the partner.

How is a marital vow implied in "leave, [...] Genesis 2:24 speaks of a "legal" process of sepa[...] ents, and the formation of a new househol[...] could "leave his father and mother," he woul[...] out the details on inheritance. He couldn't just [...] parents. A legal "transition" from the "old hou[...] quiring an official ceremony.

Here is where the oath comes into play. [...] would release their children, a legal pledge [...] made. Perhaps some symbolic gesture would al[...] In our day, the wedding ring is a token of the [...] cultures, we don't put rings in people's noses, [...] pigs or cows, but the meaning is the same. Ea[...] over the other's behavior. Thus, Moses' descrip[...] tions, received through some legal and official [...]

5. *Continuity* (Genesis 2:25). Continuity [...]

Summary

What have I covered in this chapter? I have tried to answer the question, "Who owns the family?"

The correct answer is *God!*

1. I began by pointing out that the Supreme Court has already recognized this "institutional" status of the family by "essentially" declaring it a covenant: a covenant created by God and patterned after His covenant with man.

2. Next, I showed that Deuteronomy breaks the covenant into five parts:

   1. Transcendence: Rising above man
   2. Hierarchy: God's authoritative chain-of- command
   3. Ethics: God's laws of faithfulness
   4. Sanctions: Special "self-maledictory oath"
   5. Continuity: Bond based on God's covenant

3. Then, I developed the parallel between God's covenant with man and the marital covenant. The Bible actually calls marriage a covenant, and the five-fold division carries through.

   1. Transcendence: Marriage created by God
   2. Hierarchy: Man is head over the woman
   3. Ethics: Family is governed by God's commands
   4. Sanctions: Marital covenant created by oath
   5. Continuity: Bond based on covenant

One other concluding point should be made. The structure of the principles of this book basically follow the covenantal pattern. Also, since Deuteronomy is the second giving of God's "Ten Commandment Covenant," the commandments themselves track this covenantal pattern *twice*. The first five commandments are God-ward, and the second five are man-ward. So, I will develop the principles two times, once in a general God-ward direction, and second with a man-ward emphasis.

In this chapter, I have concentrated on the fact that marriage is a "Divinely created bond," and not just an invention of man. Although the entire covenant model has been presented, it has

served the basic purpose of proving that marriage is a sacred covenant, also the first point in the five-fold structure: *Transcendence*.
So, God owns the family.

But now we want to move on to the second principle. The next
question we want to answer is, "By whose authority?" Whose authority controls the family? By whose authority can parents educate children? Is it the State's? Is it the family's? Whose is it?

Let us turn to the next chapter and answer these questions.

2

BY WHOSE AUTHORITY?

Who or what has authority over the family?
The State? The Church? The family itself?

The whole question of authority has been a big issue in the area of education. Unfortunately, controversies in the public school systems have been determining *parental authority*.

In 1985 a huge dispute in the State of New Jersey was ruled on by the Supreme Court. It seems one of the teachers went too far in searching a student. The parents complained and eventually the matter ended up in court, *New Jersey v. T.L.O.* The decision of the case restricted public school officials.

Sounds good! But wait till you hear how the public schools were limited: not by the prior authority of parents, but by the more important authority of the civil government in general. Here is part of what the court said through Judge White:

"Teachers and school administrators, it is said, act *in loco parentis* in their dealing with students: Their authority is that of the parent, not the State. . . . Such reasoning is in tension with contemporary reality and the teachings of the court. . . . If school authorities are state actors for purposes of the constitutional guarantees of freedom of expression and due process, it is difficult to understand why they should be deemed to be exercising parental rather than public authority when conducting searches of their students.

"More generally, the Court has recognized that 'the concept of parental obligation' as a source of school authority is not entirely 'consonant with compulsory education laws.'. . . Today's public

15

school officials do not merely exercise authority voluntarily conferred on them by individual parents; rather, they act in furtherance of publicly mandated educational and disciplinary policies . . . [S]chool officials act as representatives of the State, not merely as surrogates of the parents . . ."

Do you see what is being ruled in this case?

Authority has shifted away from the *parent* to the *State*. Of course, anyone who puts his child in a public school has already granted such authority to the civil government implicitly. But this case sets precedent for everyone else in New Jersey. And we can be sure that other states will appeal to this decision.

By whose authority? The State has recently ruled that the authority is the State's. The authority shift challenges the parents.

New Rights For Children
(As summarized by John Whitehead in *Parent's Rights*, pp. 24-25)

Richard Farson's *Birthrights* lists ten rights for children that are phrased to be a *direct attack on parental authority*.

1. *The Right to Self-Determination*: Children should have the right to decide matters that affect them most directly.
2. *The Right to Alternate Home Environment*: Self-determining children should be able to choose from among a variety of arrangements; residences operated by children, child-exchange programs, twenty-four hour child-care centers, and various kinds of schools and employment opportunities.
3. *The Right to Responsive Design*: Society must accommodate itself to children's size and to their need for safe space.
4. *The Right to Information*: A child must have the right to all information ordinarily available to adults—including, and perhaps especially, information that makes adults uncomfortable.
5. *The Right to Educate Oneself*: Children should be free to design their own education, choosing from among many options the kinds of learning experiences they want, including the option not to attend any kind of school.
6. *The Right to Freedom from Physical Punishment*: Children should live free of physical threat from those who are larger and more powerful than they.
7. *The Right to Sexual Freedom*: Children should have the right to conduct their sexual lives with no more restriction than adults.

8. *The Right to Economic Power*: Children should have the right to work, to acquire and manage money, to receive equal pay for equal work, to choose trade apprenticeship as an alternative to school, to gain promotion to leadership positions, to own property, to develop a credit record, to enter into binding contracts, to engage in enterprise, to obtain guaranteed support apart from the family, to achieve financial independence.

9. *The Right to Political Power*: Children must possess the same political rights as adults, such as voting, holding office and the like.

10. *The Right to Justice*: Children must have the guarantee of a fair trial with due process of law, an advocate to protect their rights against parents as well as the system, and a uniform standard of detention.

What's wrong with this list of children's "rights"? For one, some of these would be agreeable to many Christians—possessing information about your children, young people being able to work, etc.—but they're all mixed up with so many items that completely shift authority away from the parents.

For another, the whole premise of "human rights" is wrong. Man lost his rights when he rebelled against God in the garden (Genesis 3). He has no claim on God for anything. Everything which man—mothers, fathers, children—has is a *gift* from God, a result of the death of Jesus Christ on the Cross (James 1:17). So the only claim children and parents can have is through Christ!

There are no "rights *to*." There are only legal immunities *from*. There are only *zones of responsibility*: individual, familistic, ecclesiastical, and civil.

Finally, authority in this ten-point system of rights shifts from adult to child. The big movement in our society is to "adultify" the child, thereby taking authority away from the parents altogether. Farson's commandments are an attempt actually to put children in authority. It is a sign of the times—bad times. We have seen times like these before in the history of God's people, times of judgment:

> I will give children to be their princes,
> And babes shall rule over them.
> The people will be oppressed,
> Every one by another and every one by his neighbor;
> The child will be insolent toward the elder,
> And the base toward the honorable (Isaiah 3:4-5).

So, where is authority? We come to the second basic principle of the covenant of marriage and the family: *hierarchy*, or authority. But, it seems the whole question of authority has become "topsy-turvy" in our society. By whose authority is the family, or anyone, called to fulfill its responsibilities?

Two Systems of Authority

There are really only two systems of authority in the world: Theism and Humanism.

Theism teaches that *God's Word* is the infallible rule of faith and life, the final authority. Jesus prayed for the Church, "Sanctify them by Your truth, *Your word is truth*" (John 17:17). What "word" was Jesus talking about? The Bible. So, *theism* places final and ultimate authority in God and His Word.

Humanism on the other hand places final authority in man. Man sits in judgment of God and all things. In the words of the French revolutionary of the 18th century, Jean Jacques Rousseau, "The voice of the people is the voice of *God*." (He was only echoing another humanist, the Roman jurist and orator, Cicero.) Catch the significance of this statement? The will of the majority is the final authority.

Humanism in its more "sophisticated" form says there are "laws of nature," or natural laws, that govern the affairs of men. Notice how even this shifts authority away from God's personal Word. Using the same rationale, one of Rousseau's contemporaries, the Marquis de Sade, justified fornication of every kind, and murder! How? He observed in *nature* that animals openly engage in sex, and murder whenever and whomever they want. So, "natural law" allows all of the corruptions that de Sade advocated.

There are really only two sources of authority in life: the Word of God, or the word of man. Authority is either recognized in God or placed in man. That's the debate that has been going on for centuries in this country. That's the crisis in our culture today.

Always before in American life there has been a sort of "Christian consensus." But it has been so long since there has been true revival in our nation that the moral consensus has shifted. Contrary to Rousseau, the majority is not always right. Christians now find themselves having to stand against human authorities, because these people and agencies are at odds with the true authority, the Word of God.

Since authority is in God (Theism), does this mean man has no authority at all? How about parents? How about the Church? How about the State? There are three important Biblical points that we should be aware of.

Biblical Authority

We speak here not just of civil government as an institution but of all institutional authority.

Representative Government

First, Biblical authority is representative. Christianity teaches that God is *Triune*: at one time (and in eternity) Three and One, often called the "One and Many." Trinitarianism has been expressed *politically* to mean that it is neither anarchical, nor tyrannical. Why? Biblical authority is *delegated*. Moses describes this kind of "representative" authority to Israel when he says,

> How can I bear the load and burden of you and your strife? Choose wise and discerning and experienced men from your tribes, and I will appoint them as your heads. And you answered me and said, "The thing which you have said to do is good." So I took the heads of your tribes, wise and experienced men, and appointed them heads over you, leaders of thousands, and of hundreds, of fifties and of tens, and officers for your tribes. Then I charged your judges at that time, saying, "Hear the cases between your fellow countrymen, and judge righteously between a man and his fellow countryman, or the alien who is with him. You shall not show partiality in judgment; you shall hear the small and the great alike. You shall not fear man, for the judgment is God's. And the case that is too hard for you, you shall bring to me, and I will hear it" (Deuteronomy 1:12-17).

These new authorities over Israel were "chosen" by the people, and then "approved" by Moses. This relationship between established authority and the people means the leaders were "representatives." *All government is representative.* America has been built on such a view of authority.

The authority of these ancient leaders was not *in* themselves. It was "external," or "objective," to them. They represented *God's authority.* Their authority was completely in terms of what God had given them. They were not to assume to themselves *final* authority, nor were they to forget that their position came from God.

Plural Governments

Second, the Bible demands a plurality of governments. Notice that there was not just "one" leader chosen by the Israelites. There was plurality of leadership. Why? Biblical religion creates a system of "checks and balances." Again, we can see the influence of the Biblical model on our own society. America, more than any other nation, emphasizes the need for constitutional "checks and balances."

The underlying premise of Biblical pluralism in government is that man is "totally depraved" in principle (though never in history, for God restrains man's sin). No one and no institution is allowed to seek absolute authority, because the very quest for absolute power corrupts men — not absolutely, for nothing man does or can try to do is absolute, but such a quest does corrupt. It is the quest to be as God, the original corruption (Genesis 3:5). Absolute power belongs only to God. So there must be a system of checks and balances.

Historically, the Christian faith has adopted a concept of *sphere sovereignty.* Sphere sovereignty says that there are *three spheres* of covenantal government in society: Family, Church, and State. Although they overlap — a member of the family is also a member of the State and may also be a member of the Church — the *governments* of these spheres are "self-contained." By this I mean, each sphere has certain governmental responsibilities that belong "exclusively" to it.

Positively, the family has a monopoly of procreation, and possesses legitimate sovereignty over children. (Children born outside of this legitimate family authority are still called illegitimate.) Negatively, the family bears the "rod." The Bible says that the "parent" can take the rod to his child. Proverbs, addressed to "fathers," says, "Foolishness is bound up in the heart of a child, but the *rod* of correction will drive it far from him" (Proverbs 22:15).

Positively, the Church has a monopoly of administering the sacraments. Negatively, only the Church is given the "keys of the kingdom." Jesus says, "I will give you (Peter representing the Church) the *keys* of the kingdom of heaven, and whatever you bind on earth will be bound in heaven, and whatever you loose on earth will be loosed in heaven" (Matthew 16:19). "Keys" lock and unlock doors. So the Church has the "delegated" authority to admit and dismiss (excommunicate) from the Church.

Positively, the State has a monopoly of providing protection unto death. Negatively, only the State can execute, or wield the "sword." When it comes to "civil" disobedience, the State is given this authority. Paul says, "For he (Civil Magistrate) is God's minister to you for good. But if you do evil, be afraid; for he does not bear the *sword* in vain; for he is God's minister, an avenger to execute wrath on him who practices evil" (Romans 13:4).

A seeming exception to this jurisdiction of the sword is the so-called "right of self-defense." It isn't an exception. Again, we should not speak of human rights; we should speak of legal immunities. There is a person's *legal immunity* against being executed for killing someone who has threatened his or someone else's life, but this "right" of self-defense—this legal immunity from the State's execution—is delegated to him by God through the State, in whose name he is acting. He is not acting as a father or as a Church officer; he is acting as an agent of the State. The State establishes limits on such actions, even in the household (Exodus 22:2-3).

This distinction is important to emphasize in our era, which is noted by a revival of radical familism or "clan-ism," in which violence-prone men defend their supposed right to execute others as an attribute of the family or some hypothetical tribal Church. I refer here especially to a minority of radical tax protestors who proclaim violence against the State in the name of theological doctrines loosely called "British Israelitism." (A frightening example of such thinking, mixed in with open racialism, is the literature written by the late Wesley A. Swift, whose writings were used to create a heavily armed paramilitary band in California in the late 1950s and early 1960s, and whose pamphlets still circulate.)

No one sphere is allowed to establish primary authority into the other sphere. Each one has certain responsibilities and privileges that the others do not. Here is the "check and balance" of "plurality" of leadership. There are three kinds of leaders: elders in the Church, fathers in home, and civil magistrates in society. Spheres limit other spheres. For example, if the State becomes corrupt, the institutional Church must be more vocal and attempt to correct the State in a lawful and prophetic way.

Layered Governments

Third, Biblical authority is *layered*. Notice in the passage from Deuteronomy that there is an "appeals" system. Again, a "check and balance" feature appears. But the "layered" effect means *no earthly authority is absolute*.

Sometimes authorities become corrupt and they have to be disobeyed by appealing to a *higher authority*, someone who can be "appealed to." Such was the case when Daniel's friends, Shadrach, Meshach, and Abednego would not bow to Nebuchadnezzar's statue of gold (Daniel 3:1-18). What happened? They were thrown into a fiery furnace (Daniel 3:19ff.). This furnace symbolized a "trial." Whose trial? God's! Although the king thought this was his judgment, God's court had been "appealed" to. The three righteous men were found innocent, and were protected.

Even the family's authority is not absolute. Early in the history of the Church, a woman should have *disobeyed* her husband! Here is the story.

> But a certain man named Ananias, with Sapphira his wife, sold a possession. And he kept back part of the proceeds, his wife also being aware of it, and brought a certain part and laid it at the apostle's feet. But Peter said, "Ananias, why has Satan filled your heart to lie to the Holy Spirit and keep back part of the price of the land

for yourself? While it remained, was it not your own? And after it was sold, was it not in your own control? Why have you conceived this thing in your heart? You have not lied to men but to God." Then Ananias, hearing these words, fell down and breathed his last. So great fear came upon all those who heard these things. And the young men arose and wrapped him up, carried him out, and buried him. Now it was about three hours later when his wife came in, not knowing what had happened. And Peter answered her, "Tell me whether you sold the land for so much?" And she said, "Yes, for so much." Then Peter said to her, "How is it that you have agreed together to test the Spirit of the Lord? Look, the feet of those who have buried your husband are at the door, and they will carry you out." Then immediately she fell down at his feet and breathed her last. And the young men came in and found her dead, and carrying her out, buried her by her husband. So great fear came upon all the church and upon all who heard these things (Acts 5:1-11).

Sapphira died because she did not *disobey* her rebellious husband. No authority is absolute, not even the father's in the household. What could she have done? She should have appealed her husband's decision to the elders of the Church. Again, all authority is *representative* (delegated), *plural* (check and balance), and *layered* (appellate). It is precisely because the father is only a "delegated" authority that she can appeal to another "delegated" authority for help.

It is important that we keep these features of Biblical authority straight. I often hear Christians try to deal with the "abuses" of the State by absolutizing the family. This plays directly into the hands of the State because it *borrows the State's presuppositions*: Human authority can be absolutized. What is the answer? A Biblical view of authority!

Parental Authority

What is the specific authority which God gives to parents?

1. God tells parents to "be fruitful, multiply, and subdue the earth" (Genesis 1:26-28.). Parents have the authority to determine how many children they will have, and to utilize them to bring the world under the dominion of Christ. Any attempt on the part of

the State to limit the number of children is actually a direct effort to stop the dominion of Christ.

2. Parents represent the Lord to their children. Paul commands the children in the Church at Ephesus, "Obey your parents in the Lord, for this is right" (Ephesians 6:1).

3. Because of this high calling given to parents, they are to "discipline" their children. We normally think of discipline only in a negative light. But in the Book of Proverbs, discipline is "instructional" (positive) and "correctional" (negative). Solomon, for example, tells fathers to take their children out to study animals, like the ants, to learn about diligence and self-discipline (Proverbs 6:6-11). But Solomon also tells parents to use the rod, as we have seen, to correct the child. So, parents have the authority to *educate* and *punish* the children God has entrusted to them.

Parents are simply *trustees* of what belongs to God. Again, I should stress that Christians have to be careful how they argue before a watching world. Their children do not belong to them, nor do they belong to the State. They belong to God! God has delegated certain authority for parents to fulfill the trusteeship delegated to them. If the State interferes, God will deal with the State!

Summary

By whose authority? By God's authoritative Word. All authority ultimately resides here, and any other authority is *derived* from God. It is precisely because God's authority is absolute that the State has no right to violate the space and territory of other spheres, either the family or the Church.

1. In this chapter, I began with the court case of *New Jersey v. T.L.O.* The point I made was that the State is trying to shift authority away from the parents, even if it has to shift to the children first. I have made three basic points about Biblical authority.

2. Second, I established that there are only two authorities: God and man. There are consequently two systems of authority: Theism and Humanism. Theism recognizes that authority is outside of man in God. Humanism tries to place authority outside of God in man and nature.

3. After developing a "Theistic" view of authority, I turned to the Bible to note three basic principles of authority.

A. Biblical authority is *representative*. All authority is delegated, not originating in itself.

B. Biblical authority is *plural*. There are checks and balances because man is totally depraved.

C. Biblical authority is *layered*. God provides for "appeals" because no one sphere of authority is *absolute*. If it were, then *it* would be God.

4. Finally, I pointed out specific parental responsibilities and privileges. Parents have every privilege the Bible gives them. They can:

A. Discipline their children according to Biblical standards (We'll come to this in principle #4.).

B. Decide how big their own family will and will not be.

C. Educate their own children according to *their choice*, home schooling or other forms of Christian education.

Of course, each family will be accountable to God for its leadership and authority. But God "entrusts" the family with this kind of Biblical authority.

In the next chapter, we want to answer the question, "By what standard?" What standard should families live by? Whose law is to be obeyed? Should Christian schools be accredited?

Should home schools seek accreditation?

Let us move on to find the answers to these questions.

3

BY WHAT STANDARD?

Attorney David Gibbs has devoted many years to defending the lawful independence of the family from encroachments by the State. He argues that Christians need to develop a clear standard of righteousness if they are to preserve the integrity of their families. To prove his point, he says the following conversation *could* take place if a Christian parent finds himself on the witness stand.

" . . . They are going to ask you this, 'Do you own a television?'

And you'll say, 'Yes I do.'

'How much did that television cost? Five hundred dollars?' 'Where do you keep that television? In the living room or in the family room?' 'Why do you keep it there?'

'We keep it there so that the most people can see it.'

'Now, answer me this about that television. Isn't it true that if you don't plug that television in and turn it on, it is inoperable? That television cannot do anything to you until you do something to it. For it to reach you, you have to make it reach you, isn't that true?'

'Yes, that's all true.'

'Having said all of that, let me ask you this, on this television, do you ever hear obscenity? Do you ever hear someone cuss?'

'Yeah . . . .'

'There's not a given evening that you can watch it, that it will not use, in your presence, profanity and obscenity.'

'Is there any nudity, or matters of pornography?'. . . 'Do you, on that television, ever see unrighteous themes exalted?'

'All the time.'

'Do you ever see righteous themes debased?'

'Yeah.'

'And you have no problem watching those and having that in your house . . . an instrument that you have to pay hundreds of dollars to get . . . that you put right in the most travelled portion of your house . . . and that you have to make it do it to you, before it can do it to you?' *'What happened to your convictions?'* "

According to Mr. Gibbs, Christians need to know *what standard they live by*, and live it as consistently as possible!

I don't think the point is whether we have a TV in our house or not. Rather, I think the issue is *by what standard?*: knowing what it is, and how to apply it without compromise in a pagan society.

But even more important is, "Who determines by what standard Christian families should live?" In 1984, there was a famous case, *Nebraska ex rel. Douglas v. Faith Baptist Church.* The pastor and parents of Faith Baptist Church were found guilty. What happened?

These Christian parents dared to tell the State that it had no right to *set the standard* for the education of their children. What did the State want to do? It said that all the teachers in this Christian school had to comply with "State regulations," meaning the teachers had to be licensed by the State. The Pastor and the parents refused, because this was a Church school, and the State had no *jurisdiction* over the Church.

Furthermore, one Christian educator—Robert Thoburn of Fairfax Christian School near Washington D.C.—likes to say, "If I comply with the State, I will have to *lower* my school's standards." As for the students' ability in this small Christian school in Nebraska, *they tested out way ahead of the "public school" kids!* So, "quality of education" was not the issue.

It usually isn't. That's why Christian education has surpassed public school education. It always has.

The real issue in Nebraska was *by what standard?* In this chapter we want to answer this question. It's the third covenantal principle of the family: ethics, meaning moral law.

By what standard should families be governed? Who sets the standard of family life? Is it the State's law? No.

The Ten Commandments

The standard is summarized by Moses. He specifically told the parents of Israel what they were to teach their children. He said,

> Now this is the commandment, and these are the statutes and judgments which the Lord your God has commanded to teach you, that you may observe them in the land which you are crossing over to possess, that you may fear the Lord your God, to keep all His statutes and His commandments which I command you, *you and your son and your grandson*, all the days of your life, and that your days may be prolonged. . . . And these words which I command you today shall be in your heart; *you shall teach them diligently to your children*, and shall talk of them when you sit in your house, when you walk by the way, when you lie down, and when you rise up. You shall bind them as a sign on your hand, and they shall be as frontlets between your eyes. You shall write them on the doorposts of your house and on your gates (Deuteronomy 6:1-9). (emphasis added)

God calls all parents to live by God's standard, the Word of God. Here is the principle. In fact, Moses was particularly commanding parents to teach their children *God's law*. In one sense, God's law is the whole Bible. In another, it is summarized in the *Ten Commandments* themselves. So that the standard is clear, let us consider some of their applications to *families*.

What we find is that the Ten Commandments are divided into two groups of five commandments each. What we also find is that both of these groups of five points parallel the five-part covenant structure that I outlined in Chapter One.

A. *First Five Commandments*

Then God spoke all these words saying,

(1) I am the Lord your God, who brought you out of the land of Egypt, out of the house of slavery. You shall have no other gods before Me.

(2) You shall not make for yourself an idol, or any likeness of what is in heaven above or on the earth beneath or in the water under the earth. You shall not worship them or serve them; for I, the Lord your God, am a jealous God, visiting the iniquity of the fathers on the children, on the third and the fourth generation of those who hate Me, but showing lovingkindness to thousands, to those who love Me and Keep My commandments.

(3) You shall not take the name of the Lord your God in vain, for the Lord will not leave him unpunished who takes His name in vain.

(4) Remember the Sabbath Day to keep it holy. Six days you shall labor and do all your work, but the seventh day is a sabbath of the Lord your God; in it you shall not do any work, you nor your son or your daughter, your male or your female servant or your cattle or your sojourner who stays with you. For in six days the Lord made the heavens and the earth, the sea and all that is in them, and rested the on the seventh day; therefore the Lord blessed the Sabbath Day and made it holy.

(5) Honor your father and your mother, that your days may be prolonged in the land which the Lord your God gives you.

B. Second Five Commandments

(6) You shall not murder.

(7) You shall not commit adultery.

(8) You shall not steal.

(9) You shall not bear false witness against your neighbor.

(10) You shall not covet your neighbor's house; you shall not covet your neighbor's wife or his male servant or his female servant or his ox or his donkey or anything that belongs to your neighbor (Ex. 20:1-17).

Commandment 1

The first part of the Biblical covenant establishes God as the ultimate authority. He owns the world. This identifies God as the source of the covenant.

The first commandment identifies God as the liberator. It teaches that God's redemption demands total allegiance. The commandment begins, "I am the Lord your God, who brought you out of the land of Egypt" (20:2). God delivered Israel from *bondage*. His demand: "No other gods" (20:3). Because God had provided salvation, Israel was to give its undivided loyalty to Him.

Two points. *First*, parents should realize that God claims their whole family, even their children, because Christ redeemed the world. "For God so loved the *world* that He gave His only begotten Son, that whoever believes in Him should not perish but have everlasting life" (John 3:16). Just as God brought Israel out of Egypt—including *families* and not just *individuals*, and thereby demanded total allegiance from every family—so Christ makes claim on the families of the world.

Paul makes this comparison when he says, "I do not want you to be unaware that all our fathers were under the cloud, all passed through the sea, all [even the children] were baptized into Moses in the cloud in the sea, all [even the children] ate the same spiritual food, and all [even the children] drank the same spiritual drink. For they drank of that spiritual Rock that followed them, and that Rock was *Christ*" (I Corinthians 10:1-4).

Parents should teach their children that they should depend on Christ because He has redeemed their world.

Second, "he who is savior has the right to demand complete devotion." The State understands this. That's why it wants to command total submission to its will, making people think that it can provide for us from womb to tomb. The best way to fight such a false god is with the true Savior and God, Jesus Christ. The correct method for fending off false gods is to train up a generation that knows the true God. Then, they will not permit the State to act like a "savior"!

Commandment 2

The second part of a Biblical covenant establishes God's authority and His required hierarchy of responsibility.

After beginning with the identification of Himself as the liberator, God then commands *worship*. Think of it. Worship is the second most important commandment: the next two being further expansions on the second, and all the rest following in priority.

Failure to worship God is worse than murder! It's worse than adultery! It's worse than stealing!

The writer to the Hebrews says, "Let us draw near (to the throne of God) with a true heart in full assurance of faith, having our hearts sprinkled from an evil conscience and our bodies washed with pure water. Let us hold fast the confession of our hope without wavering, for He who promised is faithful. And let us consider one another in order to stir up love and good works, *not forsaking the assembling of ourselves together* (in worship), as is the manner of some, but exhorting one another, and so much the more as you see the Day approaching" (Hebrews 10:22-25). (emphasis added)

The highest privilege of every family is worship. Parents should take their children to Church so that they can worship as a family. The family that "prays together stays together." But families should also worship together in the home. Worship should be at the top of activities for the family.

Commandment 3

The third section of a Biblical covenant establishes the principles of obedience. It is concerned with law.

This commandment is a little more difficult to apply. God says that His name should not be taken in "vain." Does this have to do with "cussing"? Although I do not think it is good to use profanity, I don't think that's what God is referring to here, except indirectly.

The same Hebrew word is used by Job when he says, "For He [God] knows *deceitful* ["vain"] men; He sees wickedness also" (Job 11:11). "Vanity" in this verse is parallel with "wickedness." So, to take the Lord's name in "vain" means to be *deceitful* with His name. How would this be done? For instance, it would mean swearing to something, and trying to add power or authority to your testimony by using God's name. You would be calling down God's authority to back up your word, as if He comes at man's beck and call. God's name cannot be *manipulated* for men's purposes.

A Biblical example is the case where some Jewish exorcists tried to use Jesus' name to cast out demons. But since God's name cannot be used "deceptively," nor should it be applied in a manipulative fashion, they were attacked by the demons. They weren't under Christ's authority, so they were using His name deceitfully in their exorcism. The demons were not deceived, however, and beat them severely (Acts 19:13-16).

The family should teach its members that God's name is not a "genie's lamp." God wants His people to "trust and obey." He cannot be manipulated by man for the purposes of man.

Commandment 4

The fourth part of a Biblical covenant is judgment: imposing sanctions. Someone has to apply God's law to specific historic situations. It is always associated with "the day of the Lord," meaning the final judgment. Exercising judgment on earth is analogous to God's announcing judgment on that final day.

The fourth commandment deals with the weekly day of the Lord, or Lord's day. In the Old Testament, this was called the sabbath. It is a day of weekly self-judgment. We examine ourselves and our previous week's work, in preparation for the next week of work. The examination is done prior to taking communion in those churches that have weekly communion, which is why they have weekly communion.

God addresses the issue of time in the fourth commandment. Man is to work six days, and worship and rest for one day. The old Puritans believed this was as much a commandment about work as it was about rest. Indeed, the whole "Protestant work ethic" is built on the strong "sabbath" emphasis of earlier "Protestant" Christians.

Are Christians still supposed to work six and rest one? The writer to the Hebrews says, "There remains therefore a rest [literally "sabbath rest"] for the people of God" (Hebrews 4:9). The big difference, however, is that the New Testament people are supposed to keep their rest on *Sunday*, the day of the Resurrection of Christ. The early New Testament Christians kept this practice according to Luke's record: "Now on the first day of the week when the disciples came together to break bread" (Acts 20:7).

From the fourth commandment, families learn two things.

One, work is good and it comes before play. Children should learn to work first and then play.

Two, it is just as important to learn how to "rest." One day a week should be devoted to worship and rest. Sunday used to be a "traditional" family-day in our society, a time when everyone relaxed. Today many stores are open 24-hours a day, seven days a week. At the present rate, our civilization is going to run itself into the ground.

In our society we find two extremes: Workaholics and "leisure-freaks." The fourth commandment curbs both.

Commandment 5

The fifth part of a Biblical covenant is concerned with inheritance. It establishes the basis of continuity over time.

The fifth commandment is primarily a commandment about *inheritance*, even though it speaks of "honoring father and mother." Notice that the promise attached to it is "that your days may be long on the land which the Lord God is giving you" (20:12).

The Apostle Paul quotes the same verse, making one slight extension. He says, "that you may live long on the *earth*" (Ephesians 6:3). See the difference? Exodus 20:12 says "land," meaning the Promised Land of Canaan. And, Paul says "earth," referring to the whole world. So, by obeying parents (Biblical ones), a rich inheritance is received. Just as Jesus said, "Blessed are the meek for they shall inherit the earth" (Matthew 5:5).

Families should be taught that God's people inherit everything. Children should be instructed that the world belongs to *them*, if they obey God. This was the attitude with which our forefathers came to this country. *This world* was theirs, and they came to claim it. Of course, the Bible also tells how the inheritance should be claimed, "Not by might, nor by power, but by the Spirit of God" (Zechariah 4:6).

This is a real "vision" for success and prosperity!

Commandment 6

We begin a repetition of the five-point covenant structure. The first commandment speaks about God's sovereignty. The sixth commandment prohibits the destruction of the *image* of this Lordship. Since man is the *image* of God, he images God's sovereignty. To murder man is tantamount to a challenge to the sovereignty of God. "Whoever sheds man's blood, by man his blood shall be shed; for in the *image of God* he made man" (Genesis 9:6).

Murder is also a threat to the family. How? The "image" of God is "male and female" together. Moses says, "God created man in His own image; in the image of God He created him; *male and female* He created them" (Genesis 1:27). Marriage images God. To murder the image of God, therefore, ultimately attacks the whole family. Long before abortion was legalized, murder was removed from the category of "capital offense." Can you see the relationship? In a society that tolerates the murder of 1.5 million unborn American babies each year, this desperately needs to be communicated.

Needless to say, the sixth commandment has been muddled in people's thinking these days. People are allowed to "kill innocent children," and politicians are reluctant to take a stand against Communist insurgents, even when they're on our own borders. But those who promote such views also cry out against capital punishment. Murderers are to be given milder sentences. Abortionists are to be left alone.

In short, the guilty are protected, while the innocent are slaughtered. We need a generation of parents to raise up a future generation of children who understand that murder is an assault on the whole family!

Commandment 7

The second part of a Biblical covenant deals with authority and hierarchy.

This commandment refers to hierarchy and responsibility in the family. Adultery has to do directly with the family. It speaks of faithfulness to marriage vows. Solomon, who was an expert on adultery—he had over 900 wives and concubines at one time[1]—

---

1. Think about it. If he collected them over a period of 40 years, he was getting married on an average of every two weeks. If it took him less time to collect them, then he was getting married even more often. His court was an open invitation to lesbianism.

has these chilling words for anyone who would consider adultery:

> The commandment is a lamp, and the law is light; Reproofs of instruction are the way of life, to keep you from the evil woman, from the flattering tongue of a seductress. Do not lust after her beauty in your heart, nor let her allure you with her eyelids. For by means of a harlot a man is reduced to a crust of bread; and an adulteress will prey upon his precious life. Can a man take fire to his bosom, and his clothes not be burned? Can one walk on hot coals, and his feet not be seared? So is he who goes in to his neighbor's wife; whoever touches her shall not be innocent (Proverbs 6:23-29).

Parents should teach their children that being faithful to marriage vows affects the whole life. It is a matter of keeping that "sacred covenant" I referred to in the first chapter. "Adultery" means just that: breaking a sacred vow. If this is not learned in family life, the whole society becomes adulterous. A nation that cheats on its wives will not be a people that keeps its word.

Commandment 8

The third part of a Biblical covenant deals with living ethically (according to God's law) and not manipulatively.

This commandment prohibits one of the most obvious forms of manipulation: theft. The Apostle Paul says a thief has two problems: "Let him who stole steal no longer, but rather let him labor, working with his hands what is good, that he may have something to give him who has need" (Ephesians 4:28). A thief needs to work and to give to another person who has need. In short, he needs to stop thinking about his needs at the expense of the needs of his potential victims; he needs to quit living by manipulation of others property and become obedient.

There is a Jewish proverb that says, "A man who will not teach his son a trade teaches him to become a thief." Labor advances dominion; theft restricts it, including theft through unlimited, un-Biblical taxation.

Families should learn to work and tithe and give to the Church. A man who will not work will not tithe. And if he will do neither, he is a master manipulator: a thief.

Commandment 9

The fourth part of a Biblical covenant deals with judgment: imposing sanctions.

This commandment has to do with not "bearing false witness," speaking of the "tongue" and its proper use. What does this have to do with sanctioning? With the "tongue," man brings a false witness and sanctions falsely. On the other hand, James says it's the *last chapter in the story of "taking dominion"*: the proper form of sanctioning. Here is what he says,

> The *tongue* is a little member and boasts great things. See how great a forest a little fire kindles! And the *tongue* is a fire, a world of iniquity. The *tongue* is so set among our members that it defiles the whole body and sets on fire the course of nature; and it is set on fire by hell. For every beast and bird, of reptile and creature of the sea, is tamed and has been tamed by mankind. But no man can tame the tongue. It is an unruly evil, full of deadly poison. With it we bless our God and Father, and with it we curse men, who have been made in the similitude of God (James 3:5-9). (emphasis added)

Families and children should learn how to control the "tongue." Children should learn there is a time to speak and not to speak. James says that a man cannot control the rest of his body if he cannot deal with his "tongue." If families want to have dominion for Christ, they will have to train the "tongue."

When the State tries to control what the parents can "teach" their children, *it* is attempting to legislate or sanction the mouth; it is endeavoring to prohibit what God tells parents to do: teach the proper use of the mind and mouth.

Commandment 10

The fifth part of a Biblical covenant deals with inheritance (continuity over time).

In this commandment, God has much to say about our neighbor's property when He says not to covet what is not ours. "Coveting" means to want something that belongs to another, and to desire it to such an extent that the covetous person might even consider theft. This commandment refers to the unlawful attempt to take another's entire "estate": wife, animals, property, house (real estate), etc. This commandment nips in the bud both theft and adultery. It acknowledges that the eye is the seat of sin, which is why Jesus warned, "If your eye offends you, pluck it out" (Matthew 5:29). If it leads you to sin, then better to be blind. In short, sin is a terrible evil, with consequences worse than blindness.

There is nothing wrong with wanting a better life. But families should teach their children that covetousness is sin. To focus on another's possessions to the extent that the covetous person considers theft or oppression of the other person's estate ("patrimony") is a soul-destroying lust. Since our culture is a welfare society, fostered by a covetous civil government, it is a world of lusting and coveting. Children should learn early on that they should work for their own possessions, and take their "eyes" off of what the other children have.

Conclusion

The Ten Commandments present a double witness to God's covenant structure. They call men to obey a God who delivers them from bondage. To refuse to obey Him is to accept moral bondage as a way of life. The task of parents is to raise up a generation that wants moral freedom to obey God. The Ten Commandments are the standard for every family.

Summary

Every family needs a standard. God's revealed standard undergirds the lawful, God-given independence of the family as a separate covenant structure.

I have tried to answer one basic question: *By What Standard?*

1. I started with the case of *Nebraska ex rel. Douglas v. Faith Baptist Church*. What was at stake? The standard by which parents are allowed to raise their children. What is the standard? The Ten Commandments.

2. I briefly summarized the commandments as they would apply to the family.

A. 1st Commandment: No other gods means God owns the family.

B. 2nd Commandment: No other worship means the family that worships together stays together.

C. 3rd Commandment: No manipulation of God's name means man is to live by obedience to God's law and trust Him for the results.

D. 4th Commandment: The family is to allow God to sanction it by submitting to God's structure of time: worship and rest one day and work the other six.

E. 5th Commandment: Inheritance comes through faithfulness.

F. 6th Commandment: An attack on man is destruction of the image of God. Since the "image" is "male and female" (family), murder is an assault on the family.

G. 7th Commandment: Adultery directly affects the marriage covenant.

H. 8th Commandment: Theft is an attempt to manipulate man. As we saw in the 3rd commandment (paralleling the 8th), man is to live by ethics not magic.

I. 9th Commandment: Children are to learn how to sanction properly. Bearing false witness is an unlawful sanction.

J. 10th Commandment: Coveting what belongs to another is an attempt to take someone else's estate.

What could be added to this ethical standard? Jesus certainly didn't try to add anything. He said, "Do not think that I came to destroy the Law or the Prophets. I did not come to destroy but to fulfill. For assuredly, I say to you, till heaven and earth pass away, one jot or one tittle will by no means pass from the law till all is fulfilled" (Matthew 5:17-18). So, when a person accepts Jesus Christ as his Lord and Savior, he accepts God's righteous standard for his life. This is the standard for all families. If they lived by it and taught their children to follow it, imagine what kind of society we would have!

Our forefathers fled to this country to be able to *keep these commandments*. Freedom to them was the liberty to obey God, not disobey Him. How things have changed! The State should not set another standard, but enforce this one. Parents ought not teach another, but train their children in this one. The standard is set by God.

In the next chapter we will move on to the whole question of discipline. One of the vital areas of the State's attack on the family is here. Who determines whether parents can spank their children? How far can parents go? Does the Bible set any guidelines for discipline of children?

Let's turn to the next chapter and find out.

4

WHO OWNS DISCIPLINE?

First, do you dare to discipline?

Second, if you do dare, will the State continue to allow you to punish your children?

Don't be too quick to answer these questions until you've heard the horrifying experience of Paul Snyder, told by John Whitehead in his excellent book, *Parent's Rights*. Mr. Whitehead is a constitutional lawyer; I have thought it prudent to quote him, word for word. Understand, I am not making up any of this. My concerns are based on a frightening legal precedent. Writes lawyer Whitehead:

"On June 18, 1973 Paul Snyder took his fifteen-year-old daughter Cynthia to the Youth Services Center of the Juvenile Department of King County Superior Court in Washington. For some time Cynthia had rebelled against her parents. As one court explained the situation:

> Cynthia's parents, being strict disciplinarians, placed numerous limitations on their daughter's activities, such as restricting her choice of friends, and refusing to let her smoke, date, or participate in certain extracurricular activities within the school, all of which caused Cynthia to rebel against their authority.

"Mr. and Mrs. Snyder hoped that the Juvenile Court Commissioner would 'resolve the family dispute by admonishing Cyndy regarding her responsibilities to her parents.' Cynthia was placed in a receiving home.

"A month later, however, Cynthia, with the help of casework-

40

ers of the Department of Social and Health Services, filed a petition in court alleging that she was a dependent child under state law. The law defined a dependent child as one under eighteen years of age:

> Who has no parent, guardian or other responsible person; or who has no parent or guardian willing to exercise, or capable of exercising, proper parental control; or . . . whose home by reason of neglect, cruelty or depravity of his parents or either of them, or on the part of his guardian, or on the part of the person in whose custody or care he may be, or for any other reason, is an unfit place for such child.

"Next, Cynthia was placed in the temporary custody of the Department of Social and Health Services, and an attorney was appointed her by the court. On October 12, approximately five months after the Snyders contacted the Juvenile Department, the Superior Court found no parental unfitness. The court ordered Cynthia to be returned to her parents' custody.

"Cynthia remained with her parents for approximately one month. After more confrontations at home, she went to Youth Advocates, a group which assists troubled juveniles. From there she was directed to the Youth Services Center.

"On November 21, 1973, a state employee of the Youth Services Center filed a petition in court which alleged that Cynthia was incorrigible as defined by the law. Under this provision, a dependent child is one under eighteen years of age:

> who is incorrigible; that is, who is beyond the control and power of his parents, guardian, or custodian by reason of the conduct or nature of said child. . . .

"Cynthia, as a result of this petition, was placed in a foster home. A hearing was held several days later in which the court held that Cynthia was incorrigible. The case was appealed to the Washington Supreme Court.

"The Washington Supreme Court . . . finding a 'total collapse' in the parent-child relationship, the *court ruled the girl incorrigible*."

Who owns discipline?

Discipline Entrusted to the Parents

Have you been able to follow what happened in the Snyder case? The "awful" parents who did not want their child to "smoke," and of all things, dared to limit their daughter's activities, were ruled unfit. So the girl and the state's officials bent the law to remove her from the parents' discipline. When one court ruled that the parents were not "unfit," and that Cynthia be returned, the girl and the state officials changed their strategy. They found Cynthia "incorrigible," so that she could flee from her parents.

This is complete perversion of Biblical law.

It is also a perversion of American civil law. It has been going on for a generation or more, quietly, and parents are unaware of the change. Then, one day, reality rushes in.

The Bible teaches that God entrusts the parents with the authority to discipline. Here we see the fourth principle of the Biblical covenant: sanctions. Parents are given the responsibility to apply *sanctions* to their children: punishments and rewards.

Should the parents find it necessary to turn the child over for the discipline of the State, the civil magistrates are supposed to support this family discipline, not attack it.

Sure, there are exceptions. Parents have no legal immunity if they threaten the lives of their children. The family isn't autonomous from God's law. *Nothing* is autonomous from God's law. But short of life-endangering physical abuse, or such perversities as forcing children into immoral and illegal activities, the State should not get involved with the family's disciplining of children until the parents invite them. Also, if a child, in other words, has committed an adult crime, then of course an adult penalty should be meted out for the adult offense. Normally, however, in the case of teenage rebellion, the parents are entitled to turn their own children over first. Here is what Moses says,

> If a man has a stubborn and rebellious son who will not obey the voice of his father or the voice of his mother, and who, when they have chastened him, will not heed them, then his father and his mother shall take hold of him and bring him out to the elders of

his city, to the gate of his city. And they shall say to the elders of his city, "This son of ours is stubborn and rebellious; he will not obey our voice; he is a glutton and a drunkard." Then all the men of his city shall stone him to death with stones; so you shall put away the evil person from among you, and all Israel shall hear and fear (Deuteronomy 21:18-21).

These words may seem hard to us in our modern society. Keep in mind two important points.

First, this law limits the family. R. J. Rushdoony in his excellent book, *The Institutes of Biblical Law*, notes that the ancient pagan world allowed the family to execute its own members (See also Carle Zimmerman, *Family and Civilization* [New York: Harper and Brothers, 1947], pp. 359-383). Biblical law, however, limits the extent to which the family should apply discipline. The power of execution is given to the other members of society, and only through the civil government. The family controls the rod until it threatens to become a sword (execution).

On the other hand, this limitation on the family's authority in the long run can protect families from rule by a "criminal class." Again we return to Rushdoony's brilliant insights. He further argues that "A family turning over its son to the law will turn over *anyone*" (p. 187). So, for the family to protect itself from a "criminal class," it must allow the State to punish its own delinquent children. It must honor God's law before it honors blood lines or family name. God's name and reputation are more important.

Just about anyone who has tried to deal with someone else's children—in a church, youth organization, etc.—knows that most parents protect their children even when they are wrong! Ironically, this kind of family protection leads to its own abuse. In particular, the family ends up being abused by the State when it attempts to offset "statism" with "familism." Such has been the case in our society. Today, the State deals with everything except immorality precisely because the family is unwilling to allow its own to be punished for wrongdoing! In other words, the family wants to place itself above the law.

Second, the death penalty is only *mandatory* in the case of one capital offense: murder. There are other capital crimes. Adultery is one of them (Leviticus 18:20). Adultery is not always punishable by death, even though the Bible allows for this punishment at the request of the injured spouse. Matthew says, "Joseph was a just man . . . and minded to put Mary away privately" (Matt. 1:19). He was "just" and able to avoid the death penalty. Obviously, the offense of adultery did not require capital punishment in this case.

As mentioned, the only exception to the "not mandatory" principle is murder. Why? Death is the *only* appropriate *restitution* in the event of homicide. So, the *incorrigible* teenager is not necessarily put to death in every case, only in an "unreformable" one probably where extreme violence would be involved.

We should also keep in mind that before Christ comes in history, *redemption* is not fully at work. The death penalty was to be more rigidly applied. But after the death of Christ, the possibility of reform is greater. A Christian approach to incorrigible teenagers should lessen the need for the death penalty. A non-Biblical humanistic approach — "children will be children" — is guaranteed to increase the need for the death penalty, if not when they are children, then later, when they become murderers.

The State should uphold the law of God in the family. Parents are not unreasonable when they expect their children, especially teenagers, to obey. Parents are not over-demanding when they demand that their children stay sober and stay away from drunkenness and drugs.

Too often, however, when the State is appealed to, *it* assumes the role of parent. In the Bible, the State carries out a penalty for the parents that they were not allowed to enforce: execution. The family is not a servant of the State. The State is to be a servant of the family.

Who owns discipline? Ultimately, "God does," as we have seen in every area. Yes, He has entrusted it to the parents, but we should keep our argument straight. Parents are given the power to punish, but the Bible lays down strict guidelines. God entrusting parents with discipline in the home does not mean they can do anything they want! There are *five Biblical methods*. Let us consider them.

Biblical Methods of Home Discipline

The Bible reasons from God's methods for dealing with His people. Since the parents represent God to the children, they should look to God's example. One Biblical writer says,

> My son, do not despise the chastening of the Lord, nor detest His correction; For whom the Lord loves He corrects, *just as a father the son in whom he delights* (Proverbs 3:11-12). (emphasis added)

Discipline and love are not mutually exclusive. Discipline is the outworking of love. As God disciplines His children, so parents should punish theirs. God disciplined Christ on the cross for the sake of rebellious mankind; this should point to the link between love and punishment. God uses *five* methods.

Verbal Discipline

God would speak to His people from the Mountain or through the Prophet. When Israel sinned against God, prophets would be sent to chastise Israel *verbally*. This is apparent in all of their ministries. They brought warnings and rebukes with the hope that nothing more would need to be done to change the direction of Israel. So, there is a place for *verbal* admonition and correction in dealing with children. As God spoke sternly, so should parents know how and when to speak with sternness.

Denial Discipline

In the curse section of Deuteronomy 28, God says He will withhold increase in produce and wealth if Israel breaks His laws (Deuteronomy 28:38). When Israel would not enter the Promised Land, God withheld it from the Nation for forty years. *Denial* is an effective way to deal with children.

My school-age children have to read one book per week and then write a book report during the summer months. Once the two oldest boys wanted to take a free Karate course at the athletic club to which we belong. They were told that they could go if their report for that week was finished. They didn't finish, so they didn't get to go.

Withdrawal Discipline

David feared one thing more than anything else—*the with-drawal of God's hand* (Ps. 119). Sometimes God would pull back from His people to show them what it would be like to be totally cut off. Thus, sending a child to his room, or from the dinner table, can be an appropriate way of punishment. This can be a dangerous method. When alone, the child will have a tendency to feel sorry for himself. So, a parent should watch for this negative reaction and be prepared to deal with it.

Corporal Discipline

Deuteronomy 28, to which I just referred, says God would bring boils and other physical calamities on Israel if she persisted in rebellion. When this principle is applied to family discipline, the Bible refers to the *rod*. The *rod* became the pre-eminent symbol for discipline. Why?

The rod represented a *zone of authority*. There are different Hebrew words for "rod" but the dominant one which controls the basic word/field is *matteh* (from *natah*, which means to strike). The *matteh* was made from a branch out of a tree. Thus, the *matteh* was an extension of the tree.

Theologically, this is quite important. The "tree" in Scripture represents God's zone of authority, life, and protection. As long as one lived under God's "tree," he had God's authority, life, and protection. The Bible constantly alludes to this imagery by describing the life of blessing as a "tree by the water" (Psalm 1), by the number of leaders who appear under a "tree" (Judges 4:4ff.), and by comparing the Kingdom of God to a tree (Luke 13:19).

Therefore, the rod is to be an extension of *God's* authority. As a matter of fact, how the parent uses the rod says much about his view of God, and conveys a whole theology to the child. For this reason, the rod must be used properly.

(1) Failure to use the rod means there is no hell, judgment, pain, or evil consequences for wrong doing. God becomes Santa Claus instead of our righteous and just Sovereign. Moreover,

failure to use the rod is the easiest course of action. When a parent disciplines his child, he is dealing with a part of himself, since the child is an extension of him—a sinful extension in this case. It reminds us of the ultimate punishment we deserve: death.

This death is only symbolic, thanks to the sacrifice of Christ on the cross. The Proverbs say, "Do not hold back discipline from the child, although you beat him with the rod, he will not die. You shall beat him with the rod and deliver his soul from Sheol" (Proverbs 23:13-14). A child without discipline becomes a person without internal checks and balances. He will grow up and not be able to handle pressure, or be able to check his own sinful behavior. The Proverbs are right when they say "spare the rod and spoil the child."

(2) The rod is used instead of the hand because it is not the parent's authority which is being implemented. It is important, therefore, that a parent not deal with his own frustration when disciplining. If the parent's authority is a reflection of God's authority system, and it should be, then discipline should be for violating God's authority. The natural tendency is not to use the rod. The child will understand this when he grows up. The Proverbs say that failure to use the rod means that the parent *hates his own child* (Proverbs 13:24). When a parent uses the rod, he shows his love. In our modern mentality, we hear the opposite.

(3) Because the use of the rod is so closely tied to the child's salvation, it is good to pray with the child after the spanking has been applied. The child should confess his sin, and the parent should pray that God will use his discipline to sanctify the child.

(4) The rod should be used in private. Public flogging was the worst form of humiliation, and could only be carried out by the civil magistrates.

(5) The rod should only be applied to the behind portions of the child (Proverbs 10:13). A parent should never strike a child in the front or the face. Why? The "face" is the place of glory in Scripture. Whippings in the face destroy dignity and this is not the purpose of discipline. (Spitting in the face was allowed only in one instance in Scripture: the childless wife of a deceased man

could spit in the face of his brother if he was required to perform the office of the Levirate, to marry her and father children in the deceased man's name, and he refused [Deuteronomy 25:9]. This was a major sin against the Old Testament covenant line.)

(6) Parents should watch for sulking. This can be a very effective passive form of rebellion. The Bible says that we are to be obedient with *joy* (Deuteronomy 28:47). It is a serious problem which expresses rebellion in a bad attitude.

Disinheritance Discipline

The fifth method of discipline, and the most severe, was *disinheritance*, or *cutting off from the family*. This method is seen in God's dealings with Cain. Cain was driven away from the family and the people of God (Genesis 4:14). In the New Testament, we see this method of discipline in the parable of the Prodigal Son (Luke 15:11ff.). When a child grows into his teenage years and becomes incorrigible, even influencing the other children the wrong way, this may be the only recourse a parent has to save his household. Of course, the child should be welcomed back if he wants to come back and live by the law of the household. This is the dramatic application of the parable of the Prodigal Son.

This method could even be applied to an adult member of the family. There was a Christian family where the father left his wife of twenty-five years, committed adultery, and left the faith. His daughter was a teenager when he left. In a few years, the daughter fell in love and began to plan the wedding. The father wanted to participate in the wedding, and give her away. This was unnerving to everyone. The mother was particularly upset. Should this father have been allowed to participate in the joy of Christian marriage as long as he was unrepentant? No. As a matter of fact, when the family would not allow him to come to the wedding, he repented! It helped him to see his eternal destiny apart from repentance!

These *five* methods of discipline provide a parent with a graduated system. The wisdom of childrearing is knowing when and how to apply them. Discipline is critical to the establishment of the Biblical covenant. For, without it, there is no law.

Notice what parents are not able to do: no torturing, nothing which is life-threatening. The Bible protects the child, as well as stipulates the methods of discipline.

What if parents abuse their rights? They can be prosecuted. But they should not be taken to court for *obeying* God's law, like the Snyder's. If we had a Biblical society, the State would punish those who *break* the law of God. I am sorry to say that we have fallen from grace.

Summary

There is hope for rebellious men because there is a clear message from God. He *disciplines* those whom He loves. He loves this nation. So, He is disciplining it and will discipline it.

The principle in this chapter has been that discipline is the Lord's, entrusted to parents in the home. ("Entrusted" implies *trusteeship*.)

1. I introduced the discipline issue with the Snyder's case. Paul Snyder was not able to discipline his daughter effectively because she found protection by the State. This is nothing short of an open attack on the family. Mr. Snyder was in no way abusing his daughter. He was simply doing what he was supposed to under Biblical law.

2. God entrusts the responsibility of discipline to the parents. Deuteronomy 21:18-21 was used.

3. The specific kinds of discipline that parents can use are:

    A. Verbal discipline
    B. Denial discipline
    C. Withdrawal
    D. Corporal
    E. Disinheritance

Other forms of discipline are given to the State and the Church. I have already mentioned this. But, what the Lord gives to the family should be upheld by the State and the Church.

In the next chapter, I want to turn our attention to the *in-*

heritance. Who owns it? Why does the State try to keep families from laying up a large estate? How do I know that this is the case? Do you want your children to carry on with the faith, and the funds you've handed down to them?

Let's read on!

5

WHO OWNS YOUR INHERITANCE?

A few years ago, I needed to put in a lawn around my house. The fellow down at the local nursery said there were two ways. I could sod, or seed.

"Which is fastest," I asked. Without any hesitation, he said, "sod."

"Which is the cheapest," I followed.

"Seed," he replied.

I preferred the sod method. But my pocketbook told me I would have to grow a lawn the slow, hard way by seed.

If I had had the money, I could have started with a better foundation for my lawn, and gotten the job done faster. That would have meant I could have gone on to the rest of the landscaping sooner.

This experience illustrates the significance of inheritance. When a man acquires an inheritance from the previous generation, provided he is not a bum, he has a *foundation* on which to build. It will not completely determine his success, but it can make him more successful. It's the difference between trying to build a lawn from scratch, or being able to build on the sod of a previous generation.

The West has been established on this rich principle. Perhaps you've heard the saying, "Don't try to re-invent the wheel." This comes from the idea that we do not have to redo everything that has been accomplished over the last 6,000 years. That means there is progress. In our day, we can build on discoveries of the past to make new advances. We don't have to start from scratch.

Whether you realize it or not, this all goes back to a very important principle of *inheritance.* And, what we find true on the larger scale, is valid on the smaller, the *family.*

The principle of inheritance, as a matter of fact, finds its origin in the family. Think what it would be like if families could build up an inheritance and send their children off into the future with the foundation of the past. It would mean that they would have a better start. Like the third man in the relay race, he has a better chance of helping his team to victory if the second man passes the baton to him ahead of the other team's second man.

Somehow, we all sort of intuit that a better start is more likely to mean a better *finish.* That is, all of us except the Federal Government. The Federal Government has decided that "in order to keep the race fair," if one runner gets too far ahead of the competition, he will be required by law to slow down before he passes the baton.

What do I mean?

For almost 80 years a new philosophy about inheritance has entered our society. It all began around the turn of the century.

Income Tax

"The Congress shall have power to lay and collect taxes on income from whatever source derived, without apportionment among the several States, and without regard to any census or enumeration" (The 16th Amendment to the Constitution of the United States).

The 16th amendment altered completely this country's view of inheritance and the family. It is not like the other court cases I've presented in this book, but it is definite *legal action* that affected family life in America.

How?

There's no better way to establish my point than to allow a statement made by President William Howard Taft, made in June, 1909, in a signed message to the Senate and House of Representatives. His statement recommended the imposition of a Corporation Excise Tax, but his comments speak to proposed income tax legislation already in existence at that early date. His comments also form the rationale for the later, actual income tax amendment of 1913.

The Federal Government was running a budget deficit. He proposed to cover the deficit by raising taxes, not by cutting expenditures. (So what else is new?) He said,

"It is the constitutional duty of the President from time to time to recommend to the consideration of congress such measures as he shall judge necessary and expedient. It is now proposed to make up the deficit by the imposition of a general income tax, in form and substance of almost exactly the same character as that which in the case of Pollock v. Farmer's Loan and Trust Co. was held by the Supreme Court to be a direct tax, and therefore not within the power of the Federal Government to impose unless apportioned among the several States according to population.

"Second, the decision in the Pollock case left power in the National Government to levy an excise tax which accomplishes the same purpose as a corporation income tax, and is free from certain objections urged to the proposed income-tax measure. This is an excise tax upon the privilege of doing business as an artificial entity and of freedom from a general partnership liability enjoyed by those who own the stock. The decision of the Supreme Court in the case of Spreckels Sugar seems clearly to establish the principle that such a tax as this is an excise tax upon privilege and not a direct tax on property, and is within the federal power without apportionment according to population. The tax on net income is preferable to one proportionate to a percentage of the gross receipts, because it is *a tax upon success and not failure.* Another merit of this tax is the federal supervision which must be exercised in order to make the law effective over the annual accounts and business transactions of all corporations.

"While the faculty of assuming a corporate form has been the utmost utility in the business world, it is also true that substantially all of the abuses and all of the evils which have aroused the public to the necessity of reform were made possible by the use of this very faculty. If now, by a perfectly legitimate and effective system of taxation, we are incidentally able to possess the Government and the stockholders and the public of the knowledge of the real business transactions and the gains and the profits of every corporation in the country, we have made a long step toward that supervisory control of corporations which may prevent a further abuse of power." (emphasis added)

In case you got lost, let me summarize the significant elements in Taft's comments. One, up to that time, taxation was assessed according to the population and had to *go through the States*. In other words, the Federal Government could not tax apart from them.

Two, Taft is really providing the rationale for a *graduated income tax*, one that taxes on "success." The more you make, the more you pay as a percentage of your income. Catch the point? Before 1913, everyone would have paid the *same amount* (for example, an excise tax or sales tax on a particular product). But the income tax is specifically directed at the successful.

Some have said this was the beginning of the "transferrable society," that is, a society where money is transferred from one segment to another. It's the Robin Hood game: take from the rich and give to the poor (minus 20% for handling). Except, there essentially were no government welfare programs in 1913 because the poor were aided through private agencies and the Church. The Robin Hood of government took from the rich in the name of the poor and gave to itself.

Three, Taft clearly understood that such taxation would require more government involvement in the lives of the populace. What he calls, "federal supervision." Indeed, the Internal Revenue Service (IRS) is an autonomous government agency that has more power than any other government organization. Before the IRS the citizen is legally guilty until proven innocent, unlike the protection he receives under common law: innocent until proven guilty.

Taft's rationale won the day. Within a few years, the 16th amendment was passed, and life changed for the family, creating a chain-reaction of events. The Federal Government went from a one billion dollar national debt in 1913 to a $17 billion national debt in 1918. So much for "balancing the budget by raising taxes."

During the period of the 1930s, instead of freeing up the common man, the government took the opportunity to seize more personal freedoms, in the United States and throughout the world. The growth of central government was a universal phenomenon in the West. Why? *Because the West was steadily abandoning the last traces of Christianity.* A new God was being worshipped; the State.

Steadily, more and more personal freedom has been taken from the people. Now, virtually everyone in our society looks to the Federal Government the way our forefathers looked to their *parents*. Here is how it changed the family.

The income tax is a tax on *success*. It means that parents could no longer hand down as much to their children. Their inheritance is being eaten into. The government, no longer the family, has become the great benefactor.

But the government, unlike the family, isn't productive. It doesn't produce anything except (rarely these days) social order. It survives by extracting wealth from others, not by creating wealth. At best, it is a referee; at worst, a parasite.

So, who owns inheritance? According to the 16th amendment of the Constitution, the government has a big part of it. In principle, it has all of it. It just depends on what the politicians can collect from the taxpayers. The limit is simple: "All the traffic will bear." The more you have, the larger the percentage the government is entitled to. Is this Biblical? Do they own your inheritance, or anybody's for that matter? As we have seen before, God owns it, but delegates it through the family.

But the fifth commandment has been rewritten: "Honor the State, that thy days may be long upon the land that the land-use planning bureaucrats temporarily assign to thee."

The inheritance problem in our nation is this: to the extent that America has turned from the God of Heaven and earth who owns the inheritance, to the same degree we find Americans have lost their legacy. See what has happened? America has turned

from the Lord and has begun to lose its blessing. Income taxation
was a curse sent by God to chasten a rebellious nation.

(As an aside, there is solid historical evidence that technically
speaking, the 16th amendment was never legally ratified. The
government simply declared that it had been ratified, despite ir-
regular voting procedures at the state level that nullified its
passage. Thirty-six states were required for its adoption. Ken-
tucky's legislature, for example, did not adopt the 16th, but its
mistakenly illegal certification was counted. When the votes are
accurately counted, it turns out that only 32 states ratified the 16th
amendment. But voters were satisfied with the announced ratifi-
cation, then as now, and nobody bothered to check its legality until the mid-1980s.)[1]

Voters have turned from the God who grants true freedom.
The heart of the Gospel is freedom. Christ said, "You shall know
the truth (Christ) and the truth shall set you free" (John 8:32).
Without the Gospel, people become slaves. What do you think
people were before missionaries brought the message of Christ to
the West? Just a horde of wandering barbarians. God delivered
the West from this oppression, and America was born out of the
legacy of the freedom of the Gospel. Today, however, Americans
want to be slaves because they have turned from Christ. Until
they turn back to Him and repent, they will remain slaves.

Slaves like taxes, just so long as they believe (mistakenly) that
the rich are paying a higher share than they are. If they can "get
even" with the rich by enslaving everyone, they will vote for
slavery every time. This is the sin of envy: destruction for the sake
of leveling the rich.

So, how do we repent? How do we recapture our inheritance?
We come to the fifth principle of the covenant of the family: *Conti-
nuity*, or *inheritance*. We must consider the Word of God to see what
God requires. Only by understanding and doing exactly what He

---

1. Bill Benson and M. J. Beckman, *The Law That Never Was* (Box 550, South
Holland, Illinois: Constitutional Research Assoc., 1985); *XVI: The Constitution's
Income Tax Was Not Ratified* (1377 K St., NW, Suite #336, Washington, D.C.:
American Liberty Information Society, 1985).

tells us can we regain our inheritance, and pass it down to our children. Let's examine several elements of the principle of inheritance.

The Principle of Inheritance

An extremely wealthy man once came to me, and wanted to know which of his children should receive his inheritance. He had one son who was very wealthy, successful, but decadent. His other son was young, energetic, poor, but committed to Christ. One of his daughters had rebelled early, but come back to the family. Another daughter had been faithful, but recently turned away from the Lord.

Which ones do you think should have received the inheritance? Do you believe they should all have received "equal" amounts? Should some have been *disinherited*? Should some have received more than others?

I told this concerned father to keep three Biblical points about inheritance in mind.

Tangible and Intangible

Inheritance is tangible and intangible. Scripture places the greater emphasis on the *intangible*, while not excluding concrete wealth.

Intangible wealth has to do with "character" and "ethics." You know the old saying, "Give a man a fish, and he'll eat for a day. Teach a man to fish, and he won't need any more gifts." It's this idea. If parents just give their children material things, but fail to teach them the basic ethical principles of life, the children will squander their wealth. That's exactly what's happening in our society.

Did you know the Bible has an entire book on the ethical principles that should be handed down to the next generation? It's called the Book of Proverbs. Most of these are written by Solomon, himself the richest man in the world in his day.

The thrust of the Proverbs is summed up by an event in Solomon's life, just after he became king. It demonstrates both tangible and intangible inheritance, and where the priority should be placed.

Now the king went to Gibeon to sacrifice there, for that was the great high place; Solomon offered a thousand burnt offerings on that altar. At Gibeon the Lord appeared to Solomon in a dream by night; and God said, "Ask! What shall I give you?" And Solomon said: "You have shown great mercy to your servant David my father, because he walked before You in truth, in righteousness, and in uprightness of heart with You; You have continued this great kindness for him, and You have given him a son to sit on his throne, as it is this day. Now, O Lord my God, You have made your servant king instead of my father David, but I am a little child; I do not know how to go out or come in. And your servant is in the midst of your people whom You have chosen, a great people, too numerous to be numbered or counted. Therefore give to Your servant an understanding heart to judge Your people, that I may discern between good and evil. For who is able to judge this great people of Yours?" And the speech pleased the Lord, that Solomon had asked this thing. Then God said to him: "Because you have asked this thing, and have not asked long life for yourself, nor have asked riches for yourself, nor have asked life of your enemies, but have asked for yourself understanding to discern justice, behold, I have done according to your words; see, I have given you a wise and understanding heart, so that there has not been anyone like you before you, nor shall any like you arise after you. And I have also given you what you have not asked: both riches and honor, so that there shall not be anyone like you among the kings all your days (I Kings 3:5-13).

If God gave you one wish, what would you ask for? Solomon was initially a faithful man. His priorities were right, at least until he started marrying foreign wives by the hundreds. He wished for wisdom. Perhaps this is the reason that God could grant him such a wish. God usually does not give people what they want until their priorities are right.

What Solomon's life demonstrates is that it is not possible to remain wise if you violate a major commandment of God, year after year. Solomon remained smart; he just lost his wisdom for a lengthy period. Wisdom is a product of obedience to God's laws; disobeying the laws is the same as becoming unwise.

Nevertheless, Solomon's inheritance was both tangible and intangible. He grew rich—rich enough to afford all those wives. The intangible initially meant more to him. He knew if he had wisdom, then he would have everything. His problem appeared when the things he could afford turned out to be forbidden.

Conditional

The second point I made to the father who asked me about his children concerned the "conditional" character of inheritance. In the same passage above, God continued, telling Solomon, "So *if* you walk in My ways, to keep My statutes and My commandments, as your father David walked, then I will lengthen your days" (I Kings 14).

God granted Solomon wisdom and wealth on the basis of his *faithfulness*. But if Solomon turned from the Lord, then he would lose his inheritance. In fact, Solomon did fall away and his kingdom was divided. After Solomon, the Book of Kings takes a sad turn of events.

Of course, the message is that Solomon is like the first Adam who allowed women to mislead him. His fall eventually culminated in the coming of Christ, the faithful Son who never disobeyed His Father.

Yet, in the I Kings 3 statement that the Lord made to Solomon, we should see that inheritance should not be given indiscriminately. All children should not necessarily receive the same amounts. Nor should all the children receive anything at all.

Only the faithful should receive an inheritance. If all the children are faithful, then all should receive equal proportion. But the point is that *faithfulness determines who receives the inheritance*.

Living Trust

Finally, I told the father that inheritance should be a living trust. Even in our day, this is called an "inter vivos" trust.

What is it?

A "living trust" is where the inheritance passes to the heirs before the death of the testator. The basis for such a concept goes all the way back to the Scripture. The patriarchs, for example, bequeathed their inheritance to the heirs before their death.

> Now it came to pass after these things that Joseph was told, "Indeed your father is sick"; and he took with him his two sons, Manasseh and Ephraim. And Jacob was told, "Look, your son Joseph is coming to you"; and Israel strengthened himself and sat up on the bed. Then Jacob said to Joseph: "God almighty appeared to me at Luz in the land of Canaan and blessed me, and said to me, 'Behold, I will make you fruitful and multiply you, and I will make of you a multitude of people, and give this land to your descendants after you as an everlasting possession.' And now your two sons, Ephraim and Manasseh, who were born to you in the land of Egypt before I came to you in Egypt, are mine; as Reuben and Simeon, they shall be mine. Your offspring whom you beget after them shall be yours, and will be called by the name of their brothers in their inheritance. But as for me, when I came from Padan, Rachel died beside me in the land of Canaan on the way, when there was a little distance to go to Ephrath; and I buried her there on the way to Ephrath (that is, Bethlehem)." Then Israel saw Joseph's sons, and said, "Who are these?" And Joseph said to his father, "They are my sons, whom God has given me in this place." And he said, "Please bring them to me, and I will *bless them*" (Genesis 48:1-9).

Did you follow what was happening? Jacob (Israel) was about to die. Before he died, however, he left his inheritance to his heirs, making his legacy a "living trust."

The advantages of a living trust are three-fold. One, the heirs usually need the inheritance more when they're young, when they don't have the "start" in life.

Two, the "living trust" approach allows the parents to give the estate *gradually* to the heirs. If a large estate is involved, the heirs can become used to the inheritance so that they don't receive everything at once. They can "grow" into the wealth.

Three, the parents can see how the heirs respond to the inheritance while they are alive. If a "progressive inheritance approach" is applied, the parents can get a pretty good idea which children will be responsible.

The "living trust" is Biblical and practical. Just like the other aspects of the principle of inheritance, it formed a guideline for the father who wanted to know which children should receive his estate.

Conclusion

The question I've answered is "Who owns your inheritance?" An inheritance is important because it gives the next generation a foundation to build on. In this chapter I have done two things:

1. I have used the 16th Ammendment to introduce the whole concept of inheritance. Since the income tax legislation of 1913, which was never legally ratified, parents have been able to give less and less to their heirs. The income tax is a tax on success. Those who are most blessed are most penalized. The government has been in a battle with the family, trying to become the "parent" of the family. Is this right? No. As we've seen time and again, the State is not supposed to be a parent. It should not threaten the existence of the family, nor take what doesn't belong to it.

2. God owns the inheritance of the family, and He entrusts it to them on the basis of three principles.

A. Tangible and intangible legacies. Inheritance is in both forms. The Bible places the greater priority on the intangible, character. We saw in the case of Solomon, however, that great tangible wealth comes when man "Seeks first the Kingdom of God" (Matthew 6:33).

B. Conditional legacies. God never gives anything without requiring faithfulness. Neither should parents. When they give an inheritance to unfaithful children, grace is cheapened. They teach that God rewards the wicked.

C. Living trusts. Biblical inheritance is given while the testator lives.

These aspects of the principles of inheritance enable parents to leave something for the future. If there is no tangible inheritance for the future, then there is less hope.

It is true that the State cannot directly tax intangible wealth, but it tries. The public school system is the major instrument of the State in taxing intangible (moral) wealth. Profit-seeking, humanist-dominated television is its ally in this effort.

A very important person in the future is the *child*. He represents the future. But in our day and time, the future is threatened because of the brutal murder of children before they are born, *abortion*. In the next chapter we want to consider "Who owns life?" The Supreme Court? The mother? Who? It's certain that everything I've said about inheritance doesn't matter if a person kills all his children before they become heirs. In a way, this is what's happening in our society. No inheritance. No heirs.

Let's turn to the next chapter to learn how to save our heirs.

6

WHO OWNS LIFE?

Babies are a wonderful part of *life*. But since 1973 in the United States, they've legally been made part of death. Their mass extermination has challenged family life in America.

At the time of the writing of this book, over 18 million human beings have been slaughtered and butchered in abortion chambers all across this land of the free—free, that is, except for unborn children.

What has happened?

To get the big picture, let us sharpen our historical focus. Until 1967, virtually every state in the union had been influenced by 19th-century abortion law reform, *led by the American Medical Association*. You know, the organization that is run (or used to be run) in terms of the Hippocratic Oath, in which practitioners for 2,500 years swore never to abort a child.

How ironic.

In the 1820s, the "human ovum" was discovered. With this discovery, it was observed that the fertilization of the ovum with sperm produced life. Before, human life was considered present by the AMA at the point of "quickening," the time when the mother felt the baby move. Not until then could the doctor be sure the mother was actually pregnant. Physicians mounted a huge campaign, what one writer has called the "Physicians' Crusade Against Abortion." Every state adopted strong anti-abortion laws as a result.

Over 100 years later, this same organization was just as strongly attacking the very laws it had helped to draft. Some say it was the thalidomide tragedy in England. Thalidomide was a tranquilizer taken by pregnant women that produced horrible deformities. Doctors in the West started calling for "eugenic" ("good race") abortions, removing before birth all "defectives."

Perhaps this was the cause for such a sweeping change. I rather think it was the influence of an "evolutionary view" of man that destroyed the notion that man is created in the image of God. Once this is lost, murder becomes easy. The sixth commandment — thou shalt not murder — loses its connection to the first principle of a Biblical covenant, the sovereignty of God.

At any rate, by the late 1960s, many states started to incorporate pro-death legislation. Planned Parenthood changed its famous 1964 statement — "Abortion kills the life of a baby, once it has begun" — to read that "abortion is necessary to *prevent* unwanted children" in 1968. By the end of 1970, 18 states had passed abortion statutes. Keep in mind, however, that these states only allowed abortion in exceptional cases

By May of 1972, the New York State Legislature repealed the permissive abortion law it had passed a couple of years earlier. Then, guess what? Governor Nelson Rockefeller, running against the majority of the legislature, *vetoed* the bill and kept the abortion chambers open. This was not surprising. The Rockefeller Foundation and the Ford Foundation poured about a quarter of a billion dollars into family planning propaganda, 1965-76, second only to the Federal Government's expenditures.[1]

What was happening? The tide was changing. I believe liberals in the judicial system knew they had to strike fast, before "John Q. Citizen" figured out what was happening. As a matter of fact, in November 1972, North Dakota and Michigan attempted to pass abortion legislation, and failed by 3:1 and 2:1 margins.

There is no question that popular consensus was turning. The liberals had tried and died in their attempt to force a new human holocaust on the public.

---

1. Julian Simon, *The Ultimate Resource* (Princeton: Princeton University Press, 1981), p. 292.

The Supreme Court

Enter the Supreme Court. Members of this elite body had wanted pro-death legislation for decades. William Douglas, appointed by Franklin Roosevelt in 1939, had made no secret that he desired to attack existing laws preventing abortion.

Their chance came with the infamous case, *Roe v. Wade*. On January 22, 1973, this court handed down and foisted on the people of this land the most damaging legislation to *life*. The states could no longer pass anti-abortion statutes. The decision illegally "legalized" murder, for murder under the U.S. Constitution can be defined and prosecuted only at the state and local level. By withdrawing the jurisdiction of local civil governments to define abortion as murder during the first six months of pregnancy, the Supreme Court thereby abolished the definition of abortion as murder altogether for these children.

The Justices ruled, "The right of privacy, whether it be founded in the Fourteenth Amendment's concept of personal liberty and restriction upon state action, as we feel it is, or, as the District Court determined, in the Ninth Amendment's reservation of rights to the people, is broad enough to encompass a woman's decision whether or not to terminate her pregnancy."

The hardening sad effects of such a decision have been felt everywhere. Unfortunately, the decision of this Court overturned every state and local law in the U.S. that prohibited abortion.

Curt Young, in his excellent book, *The Least of These*, summarizes the Court's determination:

1. During the first third of pregnancy, abortion is legal for any reason as long as a licensed physician performs the procedure.
2. During the middle third of pregnancy, abortion also is legal for any reason, but states may pass laws intended to protect the health of the mother. This is a concession to the fact women face increased risk of medical complications from abortion as their pregnancy progresses. Thus, states may require that these abortions be performed in facilities with medical equipment for emergencies.

3. During the last months of pregnancy, when the baby is clearly able to survive outside the womb—is viable—if given the best medical treatment available, the Court ruled that a state "may, if it chooses, regulate, and even proscribe, abortion except where it is necessary, in appropriate medical judgment, for the preservation of the life or health of the mother."

Some Effects

How did all of this affect the family?

Listen to Linda Bird Francke, an editor for *Newsweek Magazine*: "There was no doubt, when I became pregnant, that life was right there, in my womb. Left undisturbed, that blob of cells and tissue would have grown into a baby. The process was beginning, and I chose to end it. . . .

"I was totally unprepared for my mounting ambivalence as the time for the abortion came closer, an ambivalence that turned into grief and guilt for a period after the abortion was over. The little ghost haunted me for about six months before it disappeared, and after it was gone, I even missed it a bit. But as my children grow and take up more and more of my time and energy, I realize emphatically that the addition of another child for me would have been negative rather than positive."

For this woman, another person's life had become worse than his death. So the execution of the innocent had become preferable to granting a continuation of the legacy of life.

It's like a conversation I had with an elderly woman who drove up next to me while I was picketing in front of the local abortion chamber.

The lady was extremely upset. I asked what was wrong. She said, "I can't believe you are out here wasting your time when you ought to be trying to persuade young girls not to get pregnant."

I told her all about different literature that our local chapter of Christian Action Council passes out in the schools. But she wouldn't hear me.

Again she said, "But you don't need to be out here. Get on over to the kids who are going to ruin their lives by getting pregnant."

I didn't know what else to say. Finally I said, "Ma'am, I guess the main difference between you and me is that you think *pregnancy is worse than death*. I believe *death is worse than pregnancy*, even if it is unwanted."

She slammed on the gas pedal, leaving me standing in a swirl of dust and smoke. Even though I was coughing, I could still manage a little smile and say to myself, "I got her."

If she refuses to change her thinking, God will get her, too, as He will get everyone who thinks as she does, votes as she does, and abandons the unborn to the medically certified butchers and boilers (saline solution abortions), as she does.

A lot of people would like to think that there is no hell. A lot of people would like to think that unborn babies are not human. It is understandable why there is a lot of overlap between these two groups of thinkers, and why there will be a lot of overlap between them in eternity.

The attitude that "pregnancy is worse than death" prevails everywhere. In 1984, the *American Life Lobby* ran the following statement, indicating some of the effects.

"101 Uses For a Dead (or Alive) Baby"

A workman in *Wichita, KS*, tossing bags of "pathological waste" into an incinerator from *Wesley Medical Center* (owned and operated by the United Methodist Church) discovered bags contained bodies of dead babies. For years the medical center had been sending remains of aborted babies to be burned along with "other trash.". . .

Milwaukee, WI: Police found four children in a parking lot behind Mill Medical Center playing with plastic jars containing aborted fetuses. "They told the officers they were throwing little people.". . . Not all bodies are "trashed." Babies' bodies are sold by the bag, $25 a batch—up to $5,500 a pound.

Sales of aborted pre-borns brought *Washington, D.C.*, General Hospital $68,000, 1966-1976. Money was used to buy TV sets and cookies for visiting professors . . .

In *Richmond VA*, abortion center used trash compactor to mash 100 babies' bodies which were tied up in plastic bags and tossed in trash bins. Dogs dragged bags away and fought over the contents. . . .

In *Cincinnati, OH*, abortuary allowed dense smoke to pour from its chimney. When firemen arrived on scene, they were told, "We're burning babies.". . .

Massachusetts Supreme Court ruled goldfish could not be awarded as prizes because that would violate the state's anti-cruelty laws. The same court upheld mandatory state funding of abortions. . . .

In *California*, babies aborted at 6 months were submerged in jars of liquid to see if they could breathe through their skin (they couldn't). . . .

An *Ohio* medical research company tested brains and hearts of 100 fetuses as part of a $300,000 pesticide contract. . . .

Dr. Jeromino Dominguez writes, "On any Monday you can see about 30 garbage bags with fetal material in them along the sidewalks of abortion clinics in *New York*."

Oddly, there are people — yes, even Christian people — who will be repulsed more by my listing of these horrors than by the horrors themselves.

The effects of abortion have been devastating. Words can hardly describe the horrors created in our society by this one piece of legislation.

In this chapter, the principle has to do with *life*. Keeping in mind the covenantal structure of the family, the principles start over, following the outline of the Ten Commandments. Remember the sixth commandment, "You shall not murder." Why does God forbid murder? Because He images His "transcendence" in man. So, the sixth commandment parallels the first, also teaching the principle of "transcendence." Since man images God, he should not destroy another human who does the same. To do so is tantamount to attempting to strike out at God. So, God speaks very clearly about how life and death are determined. Here is perhaps the most damaging effect of *Roe v. Wade*.

Due Process

The infamous decision affected our *entire judicial system*.
What do I mean?
The common law principle of innocent until proven guilty has been reversed. It's not just that you're guilty until proven inno-

cent. It's that you're guilty if you can be proven innocent. The acts of unborn babies are neutral before God (**Romans 9**) — man's only period of neutral acts. Yet it is only after they are born, and begin to be accountable for their external actions before God, that American civil law protects their lives.

In our land, a person is supposed to be guaranteed a *trial by jury* before he is executed. This points to the principle I'm trying to underscore in this chapter. *God owns life*, not man. The whole notion of a trial by jury originated from the Biblical concept of due process. In other words, God owns life and a trial by jury is a "check and balance" to make sure God's judgments are carried out. Instead, modern law has shifted away from any acknowledgement of an *Absolute Standard*. The Supreme Court has placed the decision of life in the hands of the mother, and taken it from God.

Now the precedent has been set. Since one group of human beings has been classified "less than human," why can't it happen to another group?

It has been discovered that in the Soviet Union, insane asylums are full of Christians, because believers in God are considered "insane." After all, they have all been educated in Marxist schools according to Marxist logic, so what else could faith in God point to, if not insanity? Logic proves atheism, so these people are dangerously illogical. They are a menace to society.

Why couldn't the Supreme Court some day decide that Christians are a "menace to the society"?

It happened before, you know: in the Roman Empire.

Biblical Law

God owns life. Only His Word should determine who can and should live.

Consider a very important passage on the subject.

> If men fight, and hurt a woman with child, so that she gives birth prematurely, yet no lasting harm follows, he shall surely be punished accordingly as the woman's husband imposes on him; and he shall pay as the judges determine. But if any lasting harm

follows, then you shall give life for life, eye for eye, tooth for tooth, hand for hand, foot for foot, burn for burn, wound for wound, stripe for stripe (Exodus 21:22-25).

What is the situation?

Two men were fighting. During the course of the scuffle, one of the men struck the wife of the other. The result was that the woman gave birth to her child "prematurely."

At this point, I will rely on James Jordan's profound commentary on these laws in his *Law of the Covenant*. Rev. Jordan says, "We have to say that there is a certain vagueness in this law, which enables it to cover several similar but slightly different situations. The particular case indicates that a bystander has been hit, but 'there is no harm.' We are not told explicitly whether the harm is to the woman or to her child, or to both, but there can be no question that the harm could be either to the woman or to her child, since both are referred to immediately prior to the phrase. Moreover, the Bible always considers the child in the womb to be fully alive, a person in the fullest sense, so that if the child came out dead or damaged, that would constitute 'harm' to the child. The situation as described in v. 22 is that the woman is late in pregnancy, and as a result of the blow is caused to deliver the child prematurely, but neither the child nor the mother is harmed by the blow.

"In this case, the husband of the woman is permitted to sue his wife's assailant in court. The judges oversee the suit to make sure that the payment required is not excessive.

"Verse 23 goes on to say that if there is harm either to mother or to child, then the assailant must pay a more severe penalty. 'Life for life' means that if either the mother or the child is killed, the assailant must also be put to death. The position of this law, after the mandatory death penalties of vv. 12-20, but before the provision for compensation in vv. 29-30, indicates that compensation is not permissible in this case."

The Bible is clear. Life in the womb is just that, a *human life*. Only God has the authority to say what should be done with this life.

Rev. Jordan goes on to make a striking application of this Biblical law to the whole question we're trying to answer.

"In either situation, the unborn child is considered a person, and is avenged. The Biblical penalty for abortion is mandatory death. The 'physician' responsible for performing the abortion is a murderer and should be put to death. Since at least two people are always involved in it, *abortion is conspiracy to commit murder,* and the 'mother,' the 'physician,' the anesthetist, the nurses, and the father or boyfriend or husband who pay for it, all are involved in the conspiracy, and all should be put to death for conspiracy to commit murder. Until the anti-abortion movement in America is willing to return to God's law and advocate the death penalty for abortion, God will not bless the movement. God does not bless those who despise His law, just because pictures of salted infants make them sick."

Exactly!

The Judge of the living and the dead condemns the judges of the infamous *Roe v. Wade.* That's why abortion is wrong. Biblical law answers the question, "Who owns life?"

Summary

1. I've attempted to answer a critical question for the family, "Who owns life?" If man does, then the family is viciously killed through the murder of its own children. I introduced the chapter with a case (*Roe v. Wade*) that illustrates this point. If God owns life, however, then the family must be protected by civil law.

In a sense, there is no question who owns the family, because there is no doubt about the Sovereign Owner of everything. God owns life. His laws are clear. A fetus is a human being. Anyone who attacks it always ends up fighting God.

2. I listed two devastating effects of *Roe v. Wade.*

  A. Pregnancy (life) is viewed as worse than death.
  B. People (unborn infants) are executed every day without due process.

3. I briefly summarized the Biblical law found in Exodus

21:22-25, which categorically condemns all of those involved in a conspiracy to murder.

Rest assured that God will win the battle. But it will be up to people who will read and believe God's Word to enforce God's law.

God's law is based on "lex talionis," an "eye for an eye." What this really means is that God *always exacts restitution*. One way or the other, God gets His restitution. It's like the old minister who preached on tithing and said, "God always gets the tithe. If He doesn't get it in money, then He gets payment in *hides*."

That's right. God always collects His restitution. One way or another, God will avenge the deaths of His innocent ones. Who knows, maybe the horrible sexual diseases (AIDS, Herpes, etc.) are a judgment on our nation for the horrible sin of abortion!

God owns life and He'll never let man forget it: One way or the other.

In the next chapter, I want to discuss the whole question of *sexual privacy*. Did you know that recent rulings on the matter directly affect your family? Want to know what they are? Want to know how to protect yourself?

Let's continue our study of "Who owns the family?" with the question, "Who owns sexual privacy?"

7

WHO OWNS SEXUAL PRIVACY?

I know, sex is one of the subjects, like religion and politics, that you're not supposed to talk about. (It's a shame that people don't *think* about religion and politics as often.)

But these days, everybody on the TV talk shows seems to be discussing the matter. So is the State.

You might be thinking, "Why in the world would the State be concerned about the issue of sex?"

I think that's a good question, because it is rather strange that the State would venture into such "private matters." What's going on? The State realizes that this is another one of those areas that determines *who owns the family.*

How so?

In *People v. Onofre* (1980), the New York Court of Appeals extended the "constitutional right of privacy" to guard the right of unmarried adults to seek "sexual gratification."

Catch the implication?

Constitutional lawyer John Whitehead, in *Parent's Rights*, explains what the whole issue of sexual privacy has to do with the family. He says,

"While sexual privacy may at first seem unrelated to the issue of family forms, this case (*People v. Onofre*) was a key factor in the subsequent decision of a lower New York court in 1981 to allow one adult male to adopt another adult male. On a variation of the privacy theory, the Pennsylvania Supreme Court has given constitutional protection to sex acts performed in a public lounge between dancing performers and lounge patrons.

"Thus, the idea of sexual privacy outside traditional marriage has, in most respects, become a part of the basic law. The older concept that such practices were to be protected only within the family unit has been eradicated.

"With the decline in the sacrosanctness of the family, however, at least two effects are evident. First, the needs of children are neglected, and as a result children are harmed. Second, *the power of the state is increased*. If these effects are not stalled, they will have a devastating impact on the stability of American society." (emphasis added)

Whitehead is absolutely right!

Here is another area that the State tries to define in an attempt to take what has been entrusted to the *family*. God created sex, so He is not against it. An entire *book of the Bible* is devoted to the subject of the sexual relationship between a man and woman, The Song of Solomon (sometimes called Canticles). He entrusts the family with this important aspect of life. It is the family that is responsible for its proper application and instruction.

Unfortunately, the war of sexual privacy is not just happening in the "civil" realm. It is also occurring in other areas.

A Newly Invented Constitutional Right

What is quite remarkable is this: there is no right of privacy listed anywhere in the U.S. Constitution! The whole doctrine has been read into the Constitution by the Supreme Court over the last two decades.

The Supreme Court enumerated this constitutional right of privacy for the first time in the landmark case, *Griswold v. Connecticut*. The state of Connecticut had made it illegal to sell contraceptives. This was challenged in the *Griswold* case, and the Supreme Court recognized a right of privacy *within the confines of marriage*, stemming from the 14th Amendment.

By 1973, this newly discovered constitutional principle had served the Court in abolishing state laws against abortion. Mothers and their licensed medical abortionists supposedly possess such a right of privacy. This "right" is outside of the jurisdictional boundary of the protection previously granted to the family in the *Griswold* case. The child who is about to be aborted is not part of this Supreme Court-invented "doctor-patient" sphere of protection.

But that was only the beginning. In that same year, University of California law professor Walter Barnett wrote a book defending the idea that state laws against homosexuality must also be abolished by this constitutional principle. His defense of this idea was financed by the taxpayers of the state of New Mexico, when New Mexico State University Press published Barnett's book, *Sexual Freedom and the Constitution*. The words on the book's front flyleaf (dust jacket flap) reveal a great deal:

"Ever since the publication of Kinsey's work on human sexual behavior in 1948 and 1953, efforts have been made periodically to revise American criminal laws on sex so as to exclude from their scope all private activity between consenting adults. Virtually none of the experts in law, the social and behavioral sciences, or psychiatry believes that legal prescription of such activity serves any justifiable purpose."

In short, the book appeals to the supposedly unanimous "experts" of the day, especially Dr. Kinsey, whose academic specialty prior to his famous books on American sexual behavior was the study of wasps. I don't mean White Anglo Saxon Protestants; I mean wasps. He had been an entomologist, not a psychiatrist. But he was accepted by the psychiatrists and other experts because they liked his conclusions, namely, that sexual deviation is so common that we can't define deviation.

What Kinsey proved was really much less significant: that *those people who were willing to fill out his questionaires* were willing to admit to deviant sexual acts. But again, the critics kept their peace: they liked his conclusions.

Then the flyleaf of Barnett's book admits a very important fact: "Almost no one has considered the possibility that reform could be compelled by the courts, through constitutional invalidation of existing laws." Remember, this was written as late as 1973.

Since that time, the supposed right of privacy, but now outside the family covenant, has been extended more widely, just as Bar-nett's book recommended, though not yet as far as he recom-mended. Prof. Barnett wanted the principle of privacy to be ex-tended all the way: "A sodomy law drawn so broadly as to apply to the consensual relations of husband and wife, as well as others, must therefore be unconstitutional." (Barnett, *Sexual Freedom and the Constitution*, p. 52. And consider this: "It should now be clear that *Griswold v. Connecticut* has opened a massive breach in the wall of traditional constitutional wisdom surrounding the sodomy laws" (p. 67). (It may be of passing interest to the reader that Prof. Barnett was a legal advisor to the U.S. State Department before he journeyed to San Francisco to join the staff at the Hastings College of Law.)

In short, the "sexual freedom" promoters argue:

1. Family government is entitled to privacy.
2. Mothers and abortionists are entitled to privacy.
3. Sodomites are entitled to privacy.

They have neglected to mention point four:

4. God is entitled to bring us AIDS.

A society that adopts Prof. Barnett's conclusion will find itself being depopulated by AIDS, as is happening today in Uganda. But that possibility didn't concern the "experts" back in 1973. And they just don't seem to mention it these days. In today's humanist-dominated world, *AIDS is a politically protected killer epidemic*.

It is my guess that it won't be politically protected forever.

War on Traditional Values

Our children are being bombarded with a set of values that is completely contrary to the traditional Biblical model. Listen to the media. Listen to spokespersons (don't you love that word, "spokesperson"?) at every level of our society, and you'll hear, "Sex in alternative forms (Homosexuality) and sex outside of marriage is OK. Maybe even A-OK."

In the *Humanist Manifesto II* it says, "We believe that intolerant attitudes, often cultivated by orthodox religions and puritanical cultures, unduly repress sexual conduct. . . . The many varieties of sexual exploration should not in themselves be considered evil. . . . Individuals should be permitted to express their sexual proclivities and pursue their life-style as desired."

The *Planned Parenthood booklet for teenagers* says, "Sex is fun and joyful, courting is fun and joyful, and it comes in all types and styles of which are okay. Do what gives pleasure and enjoy what gives pleasure, and ask for what gives pleasure. Don't rob yourself of joy by focusing on old-fashioned ideas about what's 'normal' or 'nice.' "

At the "Sex Educators Workshop" in Washington D.C., 11/81, it was said, "Parents with traditional values are 'intolerant, ignorant and bigoted'. . . Sex educators approach the following with an 'openness' to 'relieve' the child's anxieties: non-marital sex, homosexuality, masturbation, abortion, contraception and incest."

Mary Lee Tatum reported on the same worskshop, "The prevailing theme . . . children from sixth grade on must have come to accept it [homosexuality] as normal". . ."a good experience is to have two 10-year-old girls 'role play' two male lovers. Parents who quote Scripture against homosexuality are 'irrational'; their minds are perverted."

After such statements as these, I think most would agree with Barbara Morris in *Change Agents In The Schools*, "The purpose of sex education is to eradicate Christian values and Christian behavior relating to sexual activity and to replace them with Humanist values and behavior."

Clearly, there is a war on the family, and sex is one of the areas being attacked. Better put, the monopoly of *marital sex* is being attacked in the name of *sex in general*. But sex in general is the problem, *if the family has a lawful monopoly over inter-personal sex.*

This gets us back to the thesis of this book, namely, that *the family is one of God's three covenantal monopolies*, along with the Church and the State. The State has a monopoly of the sword. The Church has a monopoly of the sacraments. The family has a monopoly over inter-personal sex.

This is what the sexual freedom crowd is desperate to deny. If it gets the other two governments to accept this doctrine, then the covenantal, legal integrity of the family is overthrown, and its claim to protection from the other sovereign governments is also overthrown.

The strategy of the humanists is clear: to create an unchallenged State monopoly. The family's monopoly is easiest to deny judicially today in the name of "the separation of sex and State," meaning the separation of anti-family sex from civil prosecution. This is being done through a coordinated campaign. It is interesting that this self-conscious campaign attacks all five parts of the Biblical covenant.

1. Defining God as autonomous man (sovereignty)
2. Defining away the family (hierarchy)
3. Defining away sexual deviation (standards)
4. Overturning laws against sexual deviants (sanctions)
5. Denying civil protection for infants (inheritance)

The humanists' tactics are clear: the family is the political weak link of today's relativistic social order, and therefore the humanists' primary political target. If they succeed in destroying its integrity as a lawful covenant monopoly, then it's "one down, one to go." The Church will be next. At the end of the process there will be only one covenantal monopoly, the State. The sword will rule all.

Does the Bible have anything to say about the proper principled defense of this humanist strategy? Yes. Scripture not only condemns sex in any form outside of marriage, it speaks very positively about sex within the confines of holy matrimony. It offers both a positive and a defensive campaign.

Sex Outside of Marriage

The Bible condemns every form of sex that is not performed in marriage.

Homosexuality and Lesbianism:

Therefore God also gave them up to uncleanness, in the lusts of their hearts, to dishonor their bodies among themselves, who exchanged the truth of God for the lie, and worshipped and served the creature rather than the Creator, who is blessed forever. Amen. For this reason God gave them up to vile passions. For even their women exchanged the natural use for what is against nature. Likewise also the men, leaving the natural use of the woman, burned in their lust for one another, men with men committing what is shameful, and receiving in themselves the penalty of their error which was due (Romans 1:24-27).

Adultery:

If a man is found lying with a married woman, then both of them shall die, the man who lay with the woman, and the woman (Deuteronomy 22:22).

Pre-marital sex with engaged and not-engaged virgins:

If there is a girl who is a virgin engaged to a man, and another man finds her in the city and lies with her, then you shall bring them both out to the gate of that city and you shall stone them to death; the girl, because she did not cry out in the city, and the man, because he has violated another man's wife. Thus you shall purge the evil from among you. But if in the field the man finds the girl who is engaged, and the man forces her and lies with her, then only the man who lies with her shall die. But you shall do nothing to the girl; there is no sin in the girl worthy of death, for just as a man rises against his neighbor and murders him, so is this case.

If a man finds a girl who is a virgin, who is not engaged, and seizes her and lies with her and they are discovered, then the man who lay with her shall give to the girl's father fifty shekels of silver, and she shall become his wife because he has violated her; he cannot divorce her all his days (Deuteronomy 22:23-29).

Incest:

None of you shall approach anyone who is near of kin to him, to uncover his nakedness; I am the Lord (Leviticus 18:6).

Bestiality:

Whoever lies with a beast shall surely be put to death (Exodus 22:19).

These are certainly the most prevalent kinds of sexual sin in our society. But why does the Bible condemn them?

Scripture makes an important comparison between God and His bride, the Church, and human marriage. Paul says,

Wives submit to your own husbands, as to the Lord. For the husband is head of the wife, as also Christ is head of the Church; and He is the Savior of the body. Therefore, just as the church is subject to Christ, so let the wives be to their own husbands in everything. Husbands, love your wives, just as Christ also loved the church and gave Himself for it, that He might sanctify and cleanse it with the washing of water by the word that He might present it to Himself a glorious church, not having spot or wrinkle or any such thing, but that it should be holy and without blemish (Ephesians 5:22-27).

So, human marriage is a reflection of the marriage between God and His people. The purpose of marriage is here, not just having children or even just finding sexual fulfillment. These are secondary purposes. The reason for marriage is to display the greatest human analogy of God's union with His bride. Any kind of deviant sexual relationship mirrors the *wrong picture of God's relationship to His bride*.

Sex is evil when it is outside of marriage between man and woman. Does this mean sex is all bad? Obviously not. God is all for sex. After all, He created man and woman with the capacity to have it. He wants man and woman to be sexually fulfilled. How do I know? We've examined sex outside of marriage. Now let's look at what the Bible says about the proper sexual relationship.

Sex Within Marriage

Sex always has to do with *authority*. Remember, the second principle of the covenant concerns a Biblical *hierarchy*: so do the 2nd and 7th commandments. But what exactly does sex have to do with authority? Sex involves submission to one's partner. The Apostle Paul says the following to the Church at Corinth:

> Nevertheless, because of sexual immorality, let each man have his own wife, and let each woman have her own husband. Let the husband fulfill his duty to his wife, and likewise also the wife to her husband. The wife does not have authority over her own body, but the husband does; and likewise also the husband does not have authority over his own body, but the wife does. Stop depriving one another, except in agreement for a time that you may devote yourselves to fasting and prayer, and come together again lest Satan tempt you because of your lack of self-control (I Corinthians 7:2-5).

God is not against sex. When confined to the covenant of marriage, sex is spiritual. Paul provides us with several controlling ideas, demonstrating the relationship between sex and *authority*.

One, there is an implicit *mutually assured dependence* created by the covenant. The woman is dependent on the man, and he is dependent on her. The man is dependent on the woman by allowing her to fill the special void in his life which was created, when God removed a rib from Adam's side to make the woman. If anything else fills that void, he is acting autonomously.

The woman is dependent on man by allowing the man to give her a *functional* definition (not ethical). This is the essence of receiving the man's name. Thus, both are dependent on each other.

If she allows another to give her definition, then, like the man, her autonomous rebellion appears. Eve allowed Satan to give her a new definition: to be as God (Genesis 3:5). She submitted to Satan ethically by eating the forbidden fruit, and she then took dominion over her husband by tempting him to defy God. They both abandoned God's ethics, and this disrupted (inverted) their God-assigned functional authority relationship.

Two, sexual submission is an authority issue. In Genesis we see that God says of the woman, "In pain you shall bring forth children; Yet your desire shall be for your husband, and he shall rule over you" (Genesis 3:16). The practical, physical result is summarized by one writer, "in place of the joy at the irreducible difference of the other, the partners experience the desire of selfish possession (Genesis 3:16). The sexual drive, which is naturally extrovert, is disturbed by a movement of introversion: Instead of turning toward the other, it turns on itself!"

In other words, the Fall of man made him turn in on himself. The sexual expression of this is masturbation and rejection of God's sexual design. Redemption brings a new extroversion in marriage so that God's people ought to have the most wonderful marriages which are filled with this sexual extroversion. If not, then *rebellion* is taking place. Where *frigidity is due to rebellion, the sexual problems are ethical as opposed to psychological.*

Three, all things are lawful in the marriage bed given the parameter of mutual submission. Variety is a blessing of God. But, a husband (or wife) should not attempt variety which is repulsive to his (her) partner. Sex is an act of submission. To attempt sexual acts in rebellion to your partner undermines the whole sexual relationship.

Four, the point of temptation comes when husband and wife abstain. Notice that abstinence is not valid for the reason of marital conflict (Paul's requirement not to abstain except for fasting and prayer). And, this implies that separation from one another physically should not be for long periods of time. Also, sex was never intended just for procreation. God wants sex to be mutually satisfying.

Therefore, sex was created by God, and designed to be a part of the marriage relationship. The physical side of "one flesh" is God's gracious provision. It is a serious matter when a couple has sexual problems, and should never be underestimated. Sex is the expression of the entire marital bond.

Any time sex is taken away from marriage, or placed outside of marriage, the family is directly being attacked by Satan. When the State allows perverted sexual relationships, it is obeying Satan, not God.

When the State attempts to educate children in sexual matters, unless it affirms the Biblical viewpoint, it is playing into the hands of the Devil. The State is not supposed to be in the "education business" anyway. Ever wonder why the State *never* defends the Biblical position in all of its attempts at "sex education"?

The State is not supposed to be in any kind of education. It would be very difficult for it to uphold the Biblical position in one area when it violates Scripture in almost every other.

God is very clear about the physical relationship between a man and woman. He condemns it when outside marriage. He commends it when inside marriage. Sex, even its education, is to be confined to the realm of the family.

Summary

What have I set out in this chapter. I've raised the question, "Who owns sexual privacy?"

I believe that this is an important issue, because the State has legislated sexual privacy away from the family. It's just one more attempt to break up traditional values so that others can be substituted. Joseph Sobran, in "What Is This Thing Called Sex," *National Review*, 1/1/81, says, "It is no accident they supplement each other (Sex ed programs and socialism) . . . The socialist project of homogenizing society demands that the family be vitiated or destroyed. This can be accomplished in good measure by profaning (marriage love) and breaking monogamy's link between sex and loyalty."

1. I began with the case of *People v. Onofre* to demonstrate the shift of sexual privacy from the home to outside of it.

2. Next, I discussed a "Newly invented constitutional right" designed to expand sexual privacy. Here I showed how the case of *Griswold v. Connecticut* paved the way for *Roe v. Wade*.

3. I talked about the war on traditional values.

4. The Bible condemns sex *outside* of marriage in all its forms: bestiality, homosexuality, adultery, etc.

5. God, however, is not down on sex. In fact, God outlines how to have a successful sexual relationship *within* marriage with the following principles:

    A. Mutually assured dependence
    B. Sexual submission is an authority issue

    C. Variety allowed in terms of mutual submission
    D. Abstinence leads to temptation

Thus, God is so much for sex that He devoted an entire book to the subject, Song of Solomon. Solomon graphically addresses the question of romance between man and woman. God is not against sex! He's all for it when done according to His Word.

So, who owns sexual privacy? The family does, because God has entrusted it to this institution and no other. Once again, we see that the State has tried to legislate against God by legalizing sex outside of marriage, and by using sex education programs in the public schools in order to change the "mind-set" of American life.

The whole discussion of sexual privacy brings us to the question of *education*. Perhaps now, you can begin to see why there is such a hue and cry from liberals (and their humanist-educated Christian accomplices) about *Christian education*. Christian education cuts off their attempt to indoctrinate the next generation.

Why? Christian education provides a different *world and life view*. In the following chapter, I want to move to the area of *education*, but not education in general. Rather, I want to answers such questions as, "How does education provide a whole world and life view? So what? What is a Christian worldview? Let's turn to the next chapter to find the answers to these questions.

8

WHOSE WORLDVIEW?

Two decades ago, fundamentalist Christians began taking their children out of the public schools. Lutherans, Roman Catholics, and Dutch Reformed parents had long maintained parochial (church-run) schools as essentially immigrant-cultural protective institutions, but evangelical Christians had always regarded the public schools as "their" schools. (The Roman Catholics had agreed with them, which is why they had set up parochial schools.)

In the mid-1960s, a growing number of evangelicals figured out what they should have known from 1830 onward: that the public schools were designed by humanists for the purpose of destroying Christian civilization. Horace Mann had said so openly when he designed them in the 1830s, and by 1965, even a few of the victims had begun to catch on.

A new Christian school starts every three days, according to one estimate. They may be small, but so are termites. Eventually, the termites win, and the house collapses. That's what's happening to public schools in America.

Within the last decade, *home-schooling* has swept across the country. Over a million families now have their children in some kind of home school program.

The public schools have taken heavy losses, because droves of the best and the brightest have left. More to the point, the *principled* and the *disciplined* have left. Public educators have become outraged.

The result: secular education has tried to stretch the compulsory education laws to force children into their schools.

How?

85

The "Failure" of the Family

The logic works this way: the State requires children to be educated; the State uses tax money to create financial institutions for these children who are compelled to be educated; the State pays, so the State can legitimately determine what gets taught; finally, all children are supposed to attend State institutions.

If something sounds wrong with this syllogism, good! To help everyone to see what's wrong with its logic, let's add the word "religious" to "education."

> The State requires children to be religiously educated; the State uses tax money to create financial institutions for these children who are compelled to be religiously educated; the State pays, so the State can legitimately determine what religion gets taught; finally, all children are supposed to attend State religious institutions.

What's wrong with this? Isn't it true that children need religious education to be good citizens? Of course it's true. We also know that some parents just won't give their children the proper religious instruction. (This inevitably assumes the existence of a God-determined definition of "proper." But it also requires an institution to enforce it. The question is: Which institution?) Furthermore, we know that other parents are thoughtless, and won't spend the money to buy good religious education for their children. Must we therefore conclude: "The State therefore needs to intervene and both compel and pay for such religious instruction"?

But, the perceptive person will conclude, "This makes the State sovereign over the family." That's exactly what it does. The integrity of the family is undermined. And the family is the institution that God has assigned for the religious instruction of children (Deuteronomy 6:6-7). It is the family which is to determine what *proper* religious instruction is for its children, for better or worse.

A perceptive person will therefore conclude: "It's not worth the risk. Don't ever allow the State to compromise the family to this extent, no matter how many parents aren't giving proper religious instruction to their children." In short, *hands off!*

The Sales Job

State education propagandists have told us that some parents will inevitably fail to teach their children the basics of ("non-religious," so-called) education. They are arguing that State compulsion is the necessary motivator, for so many parents will otherwise fail to act responsibly that the State is forced to create a compulsory school system.

Let me ask you a question: How could anyone sell this idea to a nation of illiterates? How could State education promoters get taxpayers to finance the schools if the taxpayers didn't believe in paying for education? It's ridiculous! The only voters who would accept such an argument *have already decided in favor of educating their children*. To get a majority behind such a program of compulsory State education, you would first have to find voters who already overwhelmingly were literate and who were interested in educating their children.

In short, the humanists made this appeal to people who had not abandoned their family responsibilities to educate their children.

Violating Sphere Sovereignty

The problem in both examples of State-financed education—religious education or day-school education—is that the *State wants to set the standard for everything, beginning with compulsory education*. If State compulsory *religious* education is wrong, then State compulsory day-school education is equally wrong. If the State shouldn't get involved in educating children religiously because this is exclusively a family responsibility, then it must also be prohibited from getting involved in day-school (or college, or university) education. The principle of family authority and family responsibility must be maintained.

(There is one legitimate exception to this prohibition: the nation's military academies. The State is buying future officers. It could probably buy them cheaper by hiring private firms owned by retired officers to perform this training, but that's a political-military decision.)

Once, however, that State compulsory education of any kind
is conceded by the Christian, he is trapped. The Christian is
already operating by the *State's standard*. Sadly, arguments in
Christian circles concerning education usually begin with the
assumption that the State can compel. But if this assumption is
abandoned, then the State is taken out of the business of education. It's standard is completely removed. Why?

Whoever writes the "compulsory education" laws will inevitably have to *define* education. State officials are just about
always going to define education in terms of State needs for
education. The only exception would be if the State officials are
Christians. If they are, then there would be no need for the State
to define anything, because they would push it out of the education business. The State simply has no Biblical justification for
"compelling" people to be educated. Tyranny is worse than education, and people educated under tyranny still have a "slave" mentality. So, if the State sets the standard, then private education is
destroyed. The question of "Who owns education" has already
been answered, and the humanist answer is the "State."

Court Case

In *Ohio v. Whisner* (1976), the State has ruled that minimum
"standards are so pervasive and all-encompassing that total com-
pliance with each and every standard by a non-public school
would effectively eradicate the difference between public and non-
public education, and thereby deprive these appellants of their
traditional interest as parents to direct the upbringing and education of their children."

In another place this same ruling also said: "The real question
here is, not what is the best religion, but how shall this best
religion be secured? I answer, it can best be secured by adopting
the doctrine of the 7th section of our own bill of rights, and which
I summarize in two words, by calling it the doctrine of *'hands off.'*
Let the state not only keep its own hands off, but let it also see to it
that religious sects keep their hands off each other. . . . This is the
golden truth which it has taken the world eighteen centuries to

learn, and which has at last solved the terrible enigma of 'church and state.'

"Among the many forms of stating this truth, as a principle of government, to my mind it is nowhere more fairly and beautifully set forth than in our own constitution. Were it in my power, I would not alter a syllable of the form in which it is there put down. It is the true republican doctrine. It is simple and easily understood. It means a free conflict of opinions as to things divine; and *it means masterly inactivity on the part of the state* except for the purpose of keeping the conflict free, and preventing the violation of private rights or of the public peace" (emphasis added by the court).

Let's consider something else. Education is not the primary issue. *Dominion* is the real point of tension. If Christians are allowed to educate their children the way God commands, then they will dominate society. Let's get this clear from the beginning. Christianity is invincible, superior to every other system of religion. Allowed to run its course, nothing can stop it. Why do you think secular educators desperately want control of Christian children? Why do you think the State runs all the schools in Communist countries?

It's a matter of indoctrinating the children of the State's enemies with a *foreign world and life view.* A world and life view is a *grid through which everything is understood.* The power to form a young person's worldview is the heart of education. This has been understood since John Dewey, one of the founders of public education, first signed and advocated the first Humanist Manifesto. It's time Christians learned this as well.

The Bottom Line of Education

The bottom line of education is the answer to this question: *"Whose world and life view?"* Christian parents are fighting an environment that imports a competing worldview called humanism. Humanists understand this point. They know if they can take children away from their Christian family upbringing, the Christian worldview can be undermined. The past 100 years of education proves the point. (The best book on this subject, a study of the 25 major pioneers of "progressive education," is R. J. Rushdoony's *The Messianic Character of American Education*, published as far back as 1963. It has now become the "Bible" of the defenders of the Christian day school.)

Christian education, whether home or school, keeps the child in a moral environment that re-enforces the complete Christian perspective. No matter how defective, the child still hears a more consistent Christian worldview.

Some people think it is better for Christians to be exposed to a humanistic worldview at an early age. I know a man who bought this "bill of goods." He took his 11-year-old son out of a Christian school and put him into the local public school. The first week of school, the English teacher assigned a theme. The students were supposed to write on a contemporary "rock star," the list having been furnished by the teacher.

The young man knew enough to perceive that his selection was limited to pagans. He asked the teacher if he could use a contemporary "Christian" singer. The teacher said "No, because you need to broaden yourself." The boy responded, "But I've never even heard some of these musicians." The teacher smiled and took the opportunity to say, "Well, you'll just have to listen to them and write about what you hear."

Why was the teacher so "inflexible"? She wanted to shatter the boy's traditional world and life view, and at age 11. Don't think public educators fail to understand this. That's why they're fighting so hard to stop Christians from sending their children through Christian education.

It's only Christians who fail to understand this—Christians who are looking for a way to justify their tuition-saving decision to place their children in a totally hostile religious and moral environment. After all, it leaves extra money for "important" things, like a new stereo system or a vaction.

Moses states clearly *whose worldview* is to be taught.

> Now this is the commandment, and these are the statutes and judgments which the Lord your God has commanded to teach you,

that you may observe them in the land which you are crossing over to possess, that you may fear the Lord your God, to keep all His statutes and His commandments which I command you, *you and your son and your grandson*, all the days of your life, and that your days may be prolonged. . . . And these words which I command you today shall be in your heart; *you shall teach them diligently to your children*, and shall talk of them when you sit in your house, when you walk by the way, when you lie down, and when you rise up. You shall bind them as a sign on your hand, and they shall be as frontlets between your eyes. You shall write them on the doorposts of your house and on your gates (Deuteronomy 6:1-9).

God has entrusted the parents with the responsibility of educating their children. The reason is that He wants His people to grow under a thorough-going Biblical world and life view. Here is the most important principle in education.

Covenantal Worldview

We need to provide our children with a Christian worldview in their education. But what is it? Remember the covenantal model I presented in the first chapter and have been following in this book? This gives us the heart of a Christian viewpoint. The third point of the covenant is *ethics*, or law. The law sets an ethical framework for learning.

Since the *center* of the covenant is *law*, let's use the whole covenantal structure to provide this ethical approach to a Christian world and life view. I can call it a *covenantal worldview*. To refresh our memory, I said there are five parts to the covenant.

1. Transcendence: God is Lord, "standing above" as the author and controller of creation.
2. Hierarchy: Authority.
3. Ethics: Faithfulness to God's holy standard.
4. Sanctions: Reward and punishment according to obedience.
5. Continuity: A *bond* created and maintained by loyalty to the covenant.

Let's see how this covenantal grid forms a world and life view for education. I will compare and contrast it with the worldview of humanism. I've used *Humanist Manifesto I & II*, because they are the "Bible" of public education. What the manifestos say in one form, the textbooks have attempted to "flesh out" in another.

Transcendence

I've already said this means "rising above." But in what sense? God "rises above" creation in that He is the Creator, distinct in His being from man. The Bible begins, "In the beginning God created the heavens and earth" (Genesis 1:1). Before this event, there was "nothing." So, God and the rest of creation are different in their very essence.

So what?

At the heart of all pagan thought is the evolutionary notion that man is becoming "God," whether we are speaking of the Greeks, Mormons, Marxists, or the *Humanist Manifesto I*. In fact, *Humanist Manifesto I* begins in Affirmation I, "Religious humanists regard the universe as self-existing and not created." Who is God according to this system of thinking? Man.

This is the heart and soul of evolutionary thought. Evolution is the heart and soul of humanistic education. Everywhere a student turns, he reads some comment that is designed to support a basic evolutionary view of life.

Humanist textbooks are laced with comments such as, "Infants can grasp an object such as a finger, so strongly that they can be lifted into the air. We suspect this reflex is left over from an earlier stage in human evolution, when babies had to cling to their ape-like mothers' coats while mothers were climbing or searching for food" (*Understanding Psychology*, Random House, 1977).

Or, ". . . Another 1.5 billion years passed. Then the era of many-celled plants and animals began. By the time another half billion years had gone by, the seas were teeming with worms, jellyfish, sponges and corals. . . . between 5 and 2 million years ago, the appearance of human beings" (*Land and People: A World Geography*, Scott-Freeman, 1982).

It stands to reason that every subject is going to touch on the question of origins. Humanists know that a person's view of creation determines his whole outlook. So should Christians. Transcendence is either placed in God or man. When transcendence is viewed in some other location than God, man becomes "God" in his own eyes. This is why Biblical transcendence is point 1 in a Christian worldview.

Hierarchy

After transcendence comes the whole question of *authority*. Christianity says that God establishes a hierarchy of authority that reflects His transcendence. These earthly "leaders" all represent Him: the father in the home, the elder (bishop or pastor) in the Church, and the magistrate in the State.

Humanism also recognizes the importance of this issue. The *Humanist Manifest II*, principle 1, says, ". . . Too often traditional faiths encourage dependence rather than independence, obedience rather than affirmation, fear rather than courage. . . ." Principle 5 also states, "We believe in maximum individual autonomy consonant with social responsibility . . . the possibilities of individual freedom of choice exist in human life and should be increased."

Public school textbooks follow this same line of thinking in numerous examples. A 1982 homemaking text says, "During early adolescence the fight for personal independence usually begins with words. Actions follow later. When teens grow big and strong enough, conflict with parents may flare up with fights that include yelling and hitting" (*Me: Understanding Myself and Others*, Bennett, 1982).

A basal reader commonly used in public schools expresses a rebellious view of authority, "think of a situation that would probably result in a difference of opinion between your parents and yourself" (*Rebels*, Ginn & Co., 1969).

An English text says, "From whom might you resent getting some unasked-for advice about how to dress, how to wear make-up, or how to behave? Why? From some teachers, from 'old-fashioned' parents, from bossy older brothers and sisters" (*Macmillan Gateway English*, Macmillan, 1970).

Authority is necessary to a proper Christian education and view. The school, acting as a surrogate parent, should reflect God's chain of command at every point. When the student responds obediently to the instructor, he should understand that he is responding to God's representative, hired by his parents. To rebel is to revolt against God. Humanism places final authority in "self." Man is believed to be autonomous and totally unaccountable. His system says there is no God, so ultimately there is no basis for submission except for brute power, tyranny or anarchy. The person with the "biggest stick" is the leader.

Ethics

Christianity teaches that God's Law is the basis of all authority and life. There is an absolute standard of right and wrong. It used to be that virtually every child learned these. Why? Children need to learn the ethical "boundaries" of life. If they don't, then they will never be able to make good decisions.

Humanism sets out to destroy the Biblical standard. It hates the Ten Commandments so badly that they are not even allowed to be posted on any public building. The *Humanist Manifesto II* says, "We reject all religious, ideological, or moral codes that denigrate the individual, suppress freedom, dull intellect, dehumanize personality."

And, in public school textbooks, there are such examples as the following from a grade 3 textbook discussing "talking about your own ideas." It says, "Most people think that cheating is wrong, even if it is only to get a penny, which is what Shan did. Do you think there is ever a time when it might be right?" (*Communicating: The Heath English Series*, 1973).

The last example typifies the way humanist education is always trying to get the student to question Christian values. Christian education, on the other hand, provides a clear-cut system of ethics, Biblical law. What is the best environment for the student? One where God's standard is constantly being challenged, or one where it is being upheld? In a day when anything but a Christian morality is present in our society, the ethical aspect of a Christian worldview is a major priority.

Sanctions

A Christian world and life view says there are consequences to any act. Obedience is rewarded with blessing and disobedience is punished. There is an "ethical" relationship between cause and effect. Moses says, "So keep the words of this covenant to do them that you may prosper in all that you do" (Deuteronomy 29:9). Again, this is one of the five most important things a person must learn in life.

Humanism, however, teaches that there are no lasting consequences to immorality, not even a hell where people are eternally punished. The *Humanist Manifesto II*, principle 3, says, "We affirm that moral values derive their source from human experience. Ethics is autonomous and situational, needing no theological or ideological sanction." Sanction. There's that word again.

One psychology text says, "If a situation pressures a person to act in a certain way, then the person is not likely to be *judged* as the cause of the act" (*Experiencing Psychology*, Science Research Associates, 1978).

No judgment? Boy, are these humanistic authors in for a big surprise when they die! The Bible emphatically teaches that there are eternal consequences. Hebrews says, "And as it is appointed for men to die once, but after this the judgment, so Christ was offered once to bear the sins of many" (Hebrews 9:27-28).

See the connection the Bible makes? If there is no judgment, then there is no real payment for sin, no Christ. That's at stake with the humanistic worldview. Christians believe that because their worldview includes real *sanctions*, there is a need for real deliverance, salvation. "No eternal sanctions—no salvation. No eternal sanctions—no need for the cross."

Continuity

The final point in the covenantal worldview speaks to everything from who lives and dies, to inheritance. Continuity is the bond between people and everything. Scripture says the bond that holds life together is the covenant. Break it, and death results, destroying the bond and incurring the judgment of God.

Let's take death as an example. God says, "Whoever sheds man's blood, by man his blood shall be shed; for in the image of God He made man" (Genesis 9:6). If a man breaks another's continuity with life by murdering him, then he has to die, losing his bond with the living.

Humanism tries to put continuity some place other than faithfulness to God's Word. Using the same example of death, the *Humanist Manifesto II*, principle 2 says, "Promises of immortal salvation or fear of eternal damnation are both illusory and harmful. . . . There is no credible evidence that life survives the death of the body. We continue to live in our progeny and in the way our lives have influenced others in our culture."

Then, in a story out of a public school, grade 5 social studies text, humanism views continuity with life and death much differently from Holy Scripture. In a tale about an Eskimo we read, "He was to save his own life by eating his wife. At first he only cut small pieces from her clothing and ate them. . . . She ran for her life, and then it was as if Tuneq saw her only as a quarry that was about to escape him; he ran after her and stabbed her to death. After that he lived on her, and he collected her bones in a heap" (*Man: A Course of Study*, 1970).

See the difference? Continuity with life is based on the Word of God in Christianity. But in pagan religions that communicate the message of humanism, like the horrible story above, continuity with life is according to disobedience. The one who breaks God's law and murders another is the one who lives.

So, the world and life view of the Bible is covenantal. The final point of God's system is continuity. Christianity teaches that the true heirs of life will be Christians. The ones who get disinherited are the unbelievers.

Summary

In this chapter, I've ventured into the heart of Christian education: the proper world and life view. Whose worldview? God's or man's?

1. I began with a discussion of the presumed "failure" of the family to educate. The State has sold the family a "bill-of-goods" in "compulsory education" laws. The State has convinced parents that *it* has the right to write these. But there could be no compulsory ed laws if there weren't parents who *already* believed in educating their children. But the key here is that the one who writes compulsory ed laws has the right to *define* education.

2. I used the *Ohio v. Whisner* court case to show that the power to define is the power to determine what world and life view will be taught.

3. The bottom line of being able to teach a certain worldview is the *moral environment* around the child.

4. I used the covenantal model to outline the proper world and life view. Along the way, I tried to use examples from public school textbooks to show that the humanistic worldview is diametrically opposed to Christianity.

But someone might raise the question, "If there is no State compulsory education, then where's the guarantee of literacy?" In other words, "Won't educational levels drop, if the State gets out of education?" And, "If the State is pulled away from the family in this area, won't the family be defenseless in our society?"

These are legitimate questions. In the next chapter we want to answer the question, "Who Protects the Family?" The State? The Church? Or, is the family left to fend for itself?

Let's see in the following pages.

9

WHO PROTECTS THE FAMILY, AND HOW?

In the course of this book, over and over again I've stressed that God owns the family, and has entrusted sacred privileges to it. Many of these responsibilities belong only to the family, and not to the other institutions of society.

But we're so used to thinking of the State as a "parent of the family" (parentiae parens), which is precisely what the State wants us to think, that we're left wondering how anything gets accomplished if the State does not hold this parental position.

For example, in the last chapter, we talked about education. For over 100 years, our nation has allowed the State to set "compulsory education" laws. Why? Good question. Have they been successful? Judging by the chart below, we've reached new lows of literacy.

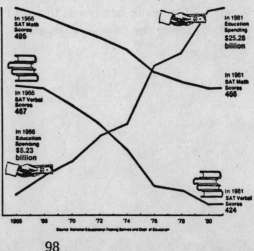

Test Scores Fall

As Aid

To Education Rises

1966-1981

In 1966 SAT Math Scores 495

In 1981 Education Spending $25.28 billion

In 1966 SAT Verbal Scores 467

In 1981 SAT Math Scores 466

In 1966 Education Spending $5.23 billion

In 1981 SAT Verbal Scores 424

Conservative Digest April 1982

1966 '68 '70 '72 '74 '76 '78 '80

Source: National Educational Testing Service and Dept. of Education

Have these State compulsory laws been effective? Have they worked? Obviously not. Let's forget about the State's ability, let alone "right," to protect the education of the family. The State has miserably failed in this area. I don't think it means that the State has no role of "protection" at all, but when it comes to education, it's not the guardian. So, with good cause, we're left asking: "Who protects the family and how?" Is the family just left to fend for itself?

Before I attempt to answer these questions, let's consider a case that will introduce several of the points I want to make.

The Quinlan Case

In the late 1970s, you may remember an important series of trials that made it all the way to the Supreme Court: The Karen Ann Quinlan case.

What were the issues?

Karen Ann Quinlan was a young girl who became comatose, through a tragic set of circumstances. She could only be kept alive by machines.

The parents wanted to turn the equipment off, because they thought *she had already died.* By law, the doctors could not allow such a thing. The family took the matter to court.

They basically argued along two lines. One, Karen had made a "living trust" with the family that if she ever became incapacitated to such an extent that she could only be kept alive by machines, they were instructed to have them *turned off.*

It seems that "in February of 1974, the father of a friend of Karen Ann Quinlan was dying of cancer. Karen, in discussion with her mother, Julia Quinlan, her sister, Mary Ellen, and her friend, Laurie Gaffney, made statements to the effect that if she were suffering from a terminal illness, she would not wish her life to be prolonged through the futile use of extraordinary medical measures."

Two, the family also argued that the trust was "sacred." Karen held her belief because the church to which she belonged (Catholic) allowed "extraordinary" means for sustaining life to be turned off.

How did the court rule?

First as to the "living trust" argument, Judge Muir said, "The preciseness of Karen Ann's state of mind is suggested to be the thing that must be in issue, and it's suggested that this is *too remote*; that there's no continuity of intent; and that there are different fact situations making it something that is not in issue." In other words, the court would not honor the statements that Karen made because it could not establish *continuity*, or a relationship between them and what actually happened to her. The "living trust" concept was rejected.

Second, the "sacred trust" approach didn't work either. Summarizing the court, it said that although the family's wishes were in "general harmony" with the Roman Catholic community, no "specific covenant" was made in the Church. If there had been, then it would have been a different matter.

What does this tell us?

The State assumes the role of "parent" above the family. Something has to challenge that role, something that has just as much power as the State, even though it may not be the same kind of power, namely the Church.

In Richard Fenn's *Liturgies and Trials*, he concludes about the Quinlan case, "The ability of an individual to challenge effectively the authority of a social system also depends on whether the individual's faith, however traditional or ancient it may be, is spoken with the authority of a particular religious community and not of the person alone."

The Church is the institution that has become a sleeping giant in our society. If it raised its head, the State would have a difficult time maintaining that "it" was the parent of the family.

Does this mean, however, that the State has no rightful place in the protection of the family? No, but its role has become confused. When it protects, it protects the wrong way. How about the Church? It's just as confused. It cowers in the corners of society, afraid to lose its 501(c)(3) status as tax-exempt. (Actually, churches are automatically tax-exempt, so by law they do not have to file for any grant of privilege under section 501(c)(3) of the Internal Revenue Code. A lot of them file anyway.)

What about the family? Cases like the Quinlans' demonstrate the need for shrewdness.

Where does this leave us? We're really touching on the fourth principle of the covenant: *sanctions*. How so? The State abuses its *sanctioning power* on the family, instead of *protecting it the proper way*. So, in our day and time the family should understand "who" and "how" protection is provided. The Bible says that each institution — Church, family, and State — protects the family in a special, but not the same way. This chapter is an attempt to present fresh Biblical information to clarify each institution's role in *protecting the family*.

The Church

The Church protects the family in a unique fashion. The institutional Church could be rightly called the "guardian of the family." Paul says,

> Honor widows who are really widows. But if any widow has children or grandchildren, let them first learn to show piety at home and to repay their parents; for this is good and acceptable before God. Now she who is really a widow, and left alone, trusts in God and continues in supplications and prayers night and day. But she who lives in pleasure is dead while she lives. And these things command, that they may be blameless. But if anyone does not provide for his own, and especially for those of his household, he has denied the faith and is worse than an unbeliever. Do not let a widow under sixty years old be taken into the number, and not unless she has been the wife of one man, well reported for good works; if she has brought up children, if she has lodged strangers, if she has washed the saints' feet, if she has relieved the afflicted, if she has diligently followed every good work. But refuse the younger widows; for when they have begun to grow wanton against Christ, they desire to marry, having condemnation because they have cast off their first faith. And besides they learn to be idle, wandering about from house to house and not only idle but also gossips and busybodies, saying things which they ought not. Therefore I desire that the younger widows marry, bear children, manage the house, give no opportunity to the adversary to speak

reproachfully. For some have already turned aside after Satan. If any believing man or woman has widows, let them relieve them, and do not let the church be burdened, that it may relieve those who are really widows (I Timothy 5:3-16).

The Church, not the State, is given the responsibility of taking care of widows. Set instructions are given. Disbursements are not to be given non-discriminately. Widows have to be a certain age, and should have demonstrated their faithfulness. The Biblical system is not a blind, "hand-out" approach. "If someone will not work, then he doesn't eat!" But why is the Church given the role of protecting and providing for the family?

Redemptive History

The Biblical history of the family sheds light on the *Church's* role.

Let's start with Genesis. The first family was told to "subdue the earth" (Genesis 1:26). Did they do what they were told? No. Adam and Eve failed and were judged, but God redeemed them. He sacrificed animals that provided atonement, or *covering*. "As for Adam and his wife, the Lord God made tunics of skin, and clothed them" (Genesis 3:21). The family would have been lost if God had not provided redemption, and pulled it back up into the Kingdom of God.

Throughout the entire Old Testament, this story repeats itself. The family falls, is judged, and redeemed. Each time, the message is: *the human family cannot save the world*. A "new" family is needed.

When you come to the time of Christ, the Gospels speak as though there is a conflict between the family and Christ. On one occasion, Jesus says,

> Do not think that I came to bring peace on earth. I did not come to bring peace but the sword. For I have come to set a man against his father, a daughter against her mother, and a daughter-in-law against her mother-in-law. And a man's foes will be those of his own household. He who loves father or mother more than Me is not worthy of Me. And he who does not take his cross and follow after Me is not worthy of Me. He who finds his life will lose it, and he who loses his life for My sake will find it" (Matthew 10:34-39).

Was Jesus doing away with the family? No. At another point in his ministry, He restored a man's child to him. It is the account of Jairus's daughter.

> And behold, one of the rulers of the synagogue came, Jairus by name. And when he saw Him, he fell at his feet and begged Him earnestly, saying, "My little daughter lies at the point of death. Come and lay Your hands on her, that she may be healed, and she will live.". . . Then He came to the house of the ruler of the synagogue, and saw a tumult and those who wept and wailed loudly. When He came in, He said to them, "Why make this commotion and weep? The child is not dead but sleeping." And they laughed Him to scorn. But when He had put them all out, He took the father and the mother of the child, and those who were with Him, and entered where the child was lying. Then He took the child by the hand, and said to her, "Talitha cumi," which is translated, "Little girl, I say to you arise." Immediately the girl arose and walked, for she was twelve years of age (Mark 5:21-42).

This healing is a symbol of *resurrection*. Notice the text says she "arose" (41,42). This is "resurrection language." Jesus' resurrection brings healing. But in this case, it is the resurrection/healing of the *family*!

So, how do we reconcile the fact that Jesus divides, yet He also resurrects the family? Just as we saw in the case of Adam and Eve, the family doesn't possess the power to save itself. This does not mean, however, that the family is done away with. No, redemption restores the family through *God's family*.

After the cross, God's "household" is the source of life for the human family. The Church, God's family, is given *guardianship over the members' families*, taking care of widows and orphans, and even providing education for families who are too poor to educate their own. Hence, churches have a legitimate Biblical place in the area of education.

The State does not have this kind of role. It cannot provide salvation for the family, nor is it supposed to assume for itself a role that belongs to the Church. But what about the State? Does this mean the State has nothing to do with the "well-being" of the family? No.

The State

The State is to protect the family by implementing the death penalty for the crimes specified in the Bible. How would this help the family?

Have you considered how capital offense crimes of the Bible are all virtually a *direct attack on the family*? Consider this as you read the Apostle Paul's list of death penalty crimes.

> Therefore God also gave them up to uncleanness, in the lusts of their hearts, to dishonor their bodies among themselves, who exchanged the truth of God for the lie, and worshipped and served the creature rather than the Creator, who is blessed forever. Amen. For this reason God gave them up to vile passions. For even their women exchanged the natural use for what is against nature. Likewise also the men, leaving the natural use of the woman, burned in their lust for one another, men with men committing what is shameful, and receiving in themselves the penalty of their error which was due. And even as they did not like to retain God in their knowledge, God gave them over to a debased mind, to do those things which are not fitting; being filled with all unrighteousness, sexual immorality, wickedness, covetousness, maliciousness; full of envy, murder, strife, deceit, evil-mindedness; they are whisperers, backbiters, haters of God, violent, proud, boasters, inventors of evil things, disobedient to parents, undiscerning, untrustworthy, unloving, unforgiving, unmerciful; who, knowing the righteous judgment of God, that those who practice such things are *worthy of death*, not only do the same but also approve those who practice them (Romans 1:24-27).

The little phrase "worthy of death" says it all. We know this means the death penalty, because Paul used the same phrase when he was accused of blasphemy. He said he had done nothing "worthy of death," meaning the *death penalty* (Acts 25:11).

Consider the effect these death penalties could have on family life in America. Murderers would be condemned to die. Child molesters would be put to death, which would mean the porno industry would die because there would not be any market. Abortion would be stopped.

Looked at in this light, is the Bible unmerciful when it speaks of death penalty crimes this way? No. The State's responsibility is to see that God's laws are applied. Its responsibility is not education. Not welfare. Not housing. Not printing money. Not 90% of what it does. All of these things have been proven to *hurt* the family. What's killing the family are the thieves and thugs in and outside of government!

But how about the family itself? Is there anything *it* can do to guard against all of the attacks on it?

The Family

Yes, the family can protect itself, but "it' ll need to be shrewd." I don't mean "illegal," but crafty in its dealings with the civil government. It will have to know the law *better than the government*. There is a good Biblical example. When the Apostle Paul was taken prisoner, he demonstrated that he knew the law of the land better than the officials who had him in custody. While standing before Festus, a Roman official, the following conversation took place.

> But Festus, wanting to do the Jews a favor, answered Paul and said, "Are you willing to go up to Jerusalem and there be judged before me concerning these things?" Then Paul said, "I stand at Caesar's judgment seat, where I ought to be judged. To the Jews I have done no wrong, as you very well know. For if I am an offender, or have committed anything worthy of death, I do not object to dying; but if there is nothing in these things of which these men accuse me, no one can deliver me to them. I appeal to Caesar." Then Festus, when he had conferred with the council, answered, "You have appealed to Caesar? To Caesar you shall go!" (Acts 25:9-12)

The Apostle Paul was a Roman citizen. He knew that he could appeal to Roman law, therefore, to receive a fair trial—anyway, more fair than he had received so far. Besides, it kept him from being murdered in Jerusalem.

Paul knew Roman law. He was not lawless or a rebel. Nevertheless, he used law to the advantage of the Kingdom of God. I believe that this is precisely what is happening in the "Christian school battle." Families have appealed to "Caesar." And, most of the time, "Caesar" is ruling in their favor. Sure, there is opposition, and it is a constant battle. But this strategy is Biblical and tried and true. (When it stops working, we can try something else.)

The family can be protected. Each sphere has a role. The Church is a guardian and provider. The State carries out the death penalty on the ones specified in God's Word, thereby "killing off" the many attackers on the family. The family itself has legal recourse by *knowing the law* better than "public school educated" state officials.

Summary

I started off by raising the question, "Who protects the family and how?"

The State and just about everyone else trying to "protect" the family are doing it the wrong way. Hence, the family goes unprotected.

1. I referred to the Karen Ann Quinlan case to show that the State reasons a certain way when it comes to protection, and anyone who wants to defend the family should take note of the issues.

2. Then I discussed how each sphere of society is supposed to protect the family.

A. The Church, not the State, is assigned the role of helping widows and orphans. Not the State. So, the Church is the check and balance on education. If you remember, at the first, I pointed out the dilemma that some think is created when state compulsory education laws are abolished. Who will fill the gap? The Church has always had the greatest interest in literacy. Why? Christianity is a religion of the *Book*! The better a person can read, the better he knows what God expects of him. Wherever Christianity has gone, therefore, literacy has followed. There is no literacy except where the Holy Spirit goes. The Church is the best guardian of education. In fact, it is the only *effective* guardian. The State needs to get out of the way of the Church if it wants a literate society.

B. When I came to the sphere of the State, I emphasized the penal sanctions of the Bible. All capital offense crimes assault the family.

C. Finally, the family defends itself by knowing the law of the land and using it to its advantage. Of course, the family should seek refuge in the Church. After all, as the Quinlan case reveals, the Church carries more clout than the individual.

Ultimately, the future is at stake. When the family is attacked, the battle is for the *children*. And, they represent the future. In the final principle, I want to consider this very important question: Who owns the children? How it is answered determines what happens to their future!

10

WHO OWNS THE FUTURE GENERATION?

He who controls the youth of this generation will dominate the next. Just about all great movements and leaders have recognized this principle. That's why Fascism invested so much in its youth during the 1930s and early 1940s, even down to the end of WWII.

In our time, there is a raging battle over who owns the *future generation*, today's children. The State would love nothing more than to capture them. But our courts answered this question a long time ago.

In 1842, the legal system of Pennsylvania had to judge an interesting case. A Mr. Armstrong had a 17-year-old daughter that a local minister wanted to *baptize*. Mr. Armstrong (a Presbyterian) argued that his daughter had already been baptized as an infant, and the minister had no right to take his daughter without his permission. In violation of the father's specific instructions, the minister baptized the girl anyway. Armstrong was so angry that he threatened the minister. The court made Armstrong put up $500 earnest money to guarantee that he would act peaceably for six months until the matter could be resolved. When it came to determining who would have to pay the court costs, the court ruled in favor of the *father*. The judge's comments reflected a very interesting understanding of the Bible.

Judge Lewis said, "It was justly remarked by Horry, Professor of Moral Philosophy, in his treatise upon that subject, that the words 'train up a child in the way he should go,' imply both the *right* and the *duty* of the parent to train it up in the right way. That is, the way which the parent believes to be right.

108

"The right of the father to command, and the duty of the child to obey, is shown upon the authority of the Old Testament, to have been established *by God Himself*. And the teachings of the New Testament abundantly prove that, instead of being abrogated in any respect, the duty of filial obedience was inculcated with all the solemn sanctions which could be derived from the New Dispensation. The fifth commandment, 'Honor thy father and thy mother,' was repeated and enjoined by St. Paul, in his Epistle to the Ephesians. Children, obey your parents in the Lord, for this is right. Ephesians 6:1."

The judge was saying that the Old Testament taught that children should be placed "in the Lord." And, the New Testament did not change this concept, because Paul says children are to be raised "in the Lord" (Ephesians 6:1), not outside of Him.

So, what's the idea?

The Generational Principle

It's the generational principle. The Bible teaches that Christianity is to grow *generation by generation*. This is the fifth principle of the covenant: *continuity*. The Church is to expand through evangelism, but it is also to grow by raising up a "holy seed."

All through the Bible, children of believers are claimed by God. Abraham circumcised his household. Moses records, "Abraham was circumcised, and his son Ishmael; and all the men of his house, born in the house or bought with money from a stranger, were circumcised with him" (Genesis 17:26-27).

The New Testament writers built on the same generational view of the faith. Luke says about the conversion of Lydia, "And when she and *her household* were baptized, she begged us, saying, 'If you have judged me to be faithful to the Lord, come to my house and stay'" (Acts 16:15). (emphasis added)

Notice that Lydia wanted them to "judge her." Why not judge everyone else in her house? They didn't need to, since they judged her. She was the adult believer, *representing* the others. She stood for her children, and they were included in the covenant because of *her* faith. She knew it, and for that reason placed her children "in the Lord."

Nowhere is this generational principle more clear than in God's words on Mt. Sinai. He says in the third commandment, "I, the Lord your God, am a jealous God, visiting the iniquity of the fathers on the children to the *third and fourth generations* of those who hate me, but showing mercy to *thousands (of generations)*, to those who love Me and keep My commandments" (Exodus 20:5-6). (emphasis added)

It takes more than one generation to build effective Christian leadership. Too often modern Christianity thinks of learning "character" in just a few years. Look at how quickly new converts are placed in positions of leadership, or even get to write books, speak, and assume any number of important responsibilities. But Scripture seems to indicate that several generations of Biblical nurture are needed to raise up effective leaders.

Often, the Bible stresses the *third* generation. Take Timothy as an example. Paul says, "When I call to remembrance the genuine faith that is in you, which dwelt first in your grandmother Lois and your mother Eunice, and I am persuaded is in you also" (II Timothy 1:5). Note the three generations: Grandmother, mother, son.

The history of Christianity has also confirmed this principle. Many, indeed most, of the great Christian leaders were not "first generation" Christians. Charles Spurgeon was the seventh generation. Charles Wesley came from a long line of Christians. Matthew Henry, author of the famous one-volume commentary, descended from several generations of faithful Puritans. Jonathan Edwards was also the seventh generation. R. J. Rushdoony is the seventh generation minister in his family. On and on the list could go.

Modern Christianity is too short-sighted. This "one-generational-thinking" was recently represented to me by a woman who said, "I don't think I need to teach my child to read because I think the rapture will take place first." With a view like this, is it any wonder the State is capturing the future generation? So, faith grows *generation by generation*, each one building and standing on the shoulders of the good work of the previous generation.

Anyone for a Covenantal Dynasty?

Scripture makes it clear that there are three ingredients necessary to build a Christian dynasty. Of Abraham, the Bible says, "For I have *known* (determined) him, in order that he may *command* his children and his household after him, that they keep the way of the Lord, *to do righteousness and justice*, that the Lord may bring to Abraham what I am doing" (Genesis 18:19). (emphasis added)

Since all true believers are Abraham's "seed" (Galatians 3:29), three relevant points stand out for us today: destiny, discipline, and dominion. God had a will and plan for Abraham that gave him *destiny*. He *disciplined* his children. And, he took *dominion* through them. Anyone who wants to extend his faith from one generation to another must inculcate these elements into the future generation.

The curious thing, however, is that non-Christians are often more successful at extending their religion and morals over the generations. Some of these families have been so successful they have become dynasties.

In May of 1979, the *Wall Street Journal* ran a series of articles titled, "Founding Families" (May 7, 1979). It was an interesting series on the great American dynasties like the Cabots, Astors, and Rockefellers. In many respects, the articles in this series are a case study of both the oddities and distinctives of these great families. Yet, I found that this series, combined with further study of dynastic families, revealed definite patterns. To the degree that a family was able to cultivate these features, it was successful in becoming a dynasty.

Destiny

First, the belief in *destiny*. The leading successful dynasties have been people of destiny—at least they perceived themselves that way. To believe in destiny means that one conceives of someone, or something, having determined his life for some *special purpose*. Whether one believes he is destined by fate, God, or chance, he thinks of himself as special.

Great men and women—Julius Caesar, George Patton, Clara Barton—have generally adhered to some concept of destiny. They saw that there was some purpose for existence which transcended their lives. Not only is this true of great men and women, but the major ideologies of the world have all held to some concept of destiny: Christianity, Islam, and Marxism. All three implicitly espouse a *doctrine of destiny*. That is, each person believes that the world belongs to him, and that some day the world will be dominated by his religion.

The concept of destiny, therefore, is not foreign to either the great individuals or ideologies of humanity. Neither is this idea alien to the great families. Among the famous American dynasties, the belief in destiny surfaces in two ways.

One, the sense of *calling*. Take the Cabot family of Boston as an example. This dynasty, like most goes back for centuries. After choosing the winning side in the Revolutionary War—it always helps to choose the winning side in anything—the Cabots built family wealth on the wide variance of calling among their children. Not just any calling, however, for child after child grew up to become a professional who riveted another pillar for his family in the community. Perhaps no other family has had such diversity of professionalism—industrialists, merchants, doctors, lawyers, architects, U.S. Senators, ambassadors, judges, and sea captains. The great wealth of the family did not emerge until the end of the 19th century. At that time, Godfrey L. Cabot founded his famous Carbon Black industry. Nevertheless, the diversity of occupational callings, and the sense of general calling, sustained the Cabot family for well over a century.

Two, *vision*. We said earlier that the man (or woman) with a sense of destiny *sees* himself (herself) as special. This sight spills over into the ability to visualize opportunity and success. Almost all of the founders of the great dynasties possessed *vision*.

Meyer Guggenheim was a man of vision. In the mid-19th century, he *saw* that the manufacturers made the big profits on the goods he was peddling. So, he started to manufacture in a small way a few items. One day, he made enough money to buy a few mines in Colorado. When his partners sold out because the mines were flooded, he knew better. He caught the vision for what lay in those mines. That vision gave birth to creativity.

He traveled to Colorado, had the mines pumped out, and founded one of the largest silver mines in Colorado. It produced $750,000 dollars the first year. What was the difference between Guggenheim and his partners? He had the vision which turned into creativity and fortitude. He was a man of destiny.

It's interesting to see how many of the great fortunes were a result of supposed "chance." The famous "Daisy Bradford" oil well in East Texas, the one which made the Hunt family fortune, is a case in point. The original site for the well was several hundred feet from the famous gusher. The story is that rain and mud kept the mules from pulling the rig to the original site. The only thing that could be done was stop the rig and sink a well at the point where the wagon could be pulled no further. Was this chance? This was destiny. The Hunt family is not yet a dynasty, since it takes at least a century to produce one. No doubt, however, they are a family of destiny. (Actually, they are two families of destiny: they came from the two wives of H. L. Hunt.) To build a great dynasty, they must recognize the fact, and reproduce this dynastic mentality in their offspring.

Discipline

Second, along with destiny, we find that discipline must accompany a sense of destiny. Guggenheim had to be disciplined enough to see the job of pumping those silver mines to the end. He had to be willing to work. Hard work built the large financial dynasties. They did not just happen.

The common man has a mythical view of the children of these dynasties. He thinks the children are lavished with wealth with which they can buy every toy available. Certainly this happens in some cases. If a family was to keep its wealth, however, the children had to learn the value of a dollar.

In fact, many of these large families have had the practice of not leaving large sums of money to the children. The general rule was, "don't leave so much money that the children have to devote full time to spending it." Many times this rule was implemented by some sort of discretionary inheritance to make the heirs earn their own way.

Godfrey Cabot, for example, did not leave his heirs a large amount of money. Why? He believed that real prosperity should come to them through their own diligence, and not through his death. Therefore, he helped them while he was alive to get started in businesses. If the effort failed, the heir didn't receive any inheritance. In other words, the faithful received the blessing. By doing this, he made them become disciplined.

Dominion

Third, the ability to dominate is the final characteristic. Many have and can make a sudden fortune, either through an inheritance, lottery, hot tip on the stock market, or other ways. But it is another matter to *stay* on top. Moreover, staying on top is difficult, but even harder is the use of wealth to dominate other people and ideas. In other words, have dominion.

The Avoidance of Corruption

In the *super*-dynasties, such as the Sassoons and the Rothschilds, discipline and dominion come together in an interesting way: the ability *to use vice without becoming addicted to vice*. This illustrates the general Biblical principle that even if men's hearts are not submissive to God, God will bless their efforts externally if they follow certain fundamental principles. The self-discipline of avoiding vice, year after year, no matter how close at hand, is one such principle.

Take the Sassoons. Stanley Jackson has written a biography on the Sassons where he calls them the Rothschilds of the East. (*The Sassoons* [New York: E. P. Dutton & Co., 1968], p. 3.) Their dynasty goes back to Sheik Sason (his descendants would use the modern variation of Sassoon) in 1778. He had risen from coin collector to the most influential banker of Baghdad. They were Orthodox Jews, like the original Rothschilds, and quite dedicated to the expansion of Judaism.

Jackson summarizes the family: "Sheik Sason supervised the secular welfare of his people but also provided funds for religious education. With the rabbis he inspected ritual baths and ensured that the slaughter-houses and dairies conformed strictly to the dietary laws. Door-posts had to be checked every three years to see that the *Mezuzahs*—tiny scrolls of the Holy Law encased in metal strips—were in good repair. Orphan girls were given dowries; rabbis, travellers, and pilgrims from the Holy Land, even from distant China, were welcomed in the Nasi's (Sheik Sason's official title) house where they took their ease in a walled courtyard shady with orange trees and shrubs" (pp. 3-4). Sheik Sason even made a point to help start a synagogue, if there were none, in every city he travelled to.

It was under this kind of discipline that his son David Sassoon began to learn the trade of his father. From his earliest age, he sat in the counting-house with his father, and learned about money, borrowing, and lending. In his case, he mostly loaned and made money.

Due to a change in local power in Baghdad, the family had to move. David was the first to leave and seek his fortune in another city. With coins sewn in the lining of his clothing, he fled for his very life. Eventually, he ended his search for a new home in Bombay, India. It was here, *through his sons*, that the great wealth of the Sassoons was achieved. Discipline leads to dominion! Jackson adds, "The cotton magnate and first Parsee baronet, Sir Jamesetjee Jejeebhoy, once declared emphatically that 'the chief cause of David Sassoon's success was the use he made of his sons.' He trained them to be chorus masters, with himself as conductor" (p. 31). The "conductor" and the "chorus masters" made the family fortunes through real estate, cotton and opium in the East.

Elias was the son of David Sassoon. Jackson refers to him as the black sheep, so to speak, and the one who seized the opportunity in the opium market (pp. 51ff.). Ironically, it is here that we learn one of the great principles of dominion in a *perverted form*.

Let's look at the perverted version first, so that we can accent the Biblical principle.

Through Elias' travels in China, he perceived (vision) that great fortunes could be made through opium. He was a rebel, and he fell out of favor, unofficially, with the family for hiring outsiders (non-Jews) in the family business. But through all of this, Elias Sassoon displayed the rare ability *to use vice without becoming addicted to vice.*

Even if Jackson happens to be wrong in his findings about the origin of the Sassoons' fortune—though this seems unlikely—we see the same principle in operation elsewhere. The Italians and Jews who immigrated to this country and became involved in organized crime illustrate the same kind of thing. All their lives, they had been served wine with meals, and learned how to drink without becoming drunkards. How did this help them to become powerful in organized crime? Thomas Sowell explains in the following description of the Italian rise to power among organized crime in the 1920s:

"Organized crime had existed in the United States before Italians became part of it. The leading gangsters were Irish or Jewish, on into the 1920s. The introduction of Prohibition greatly increased the scope of organized crime in the United States, at about the same time that Italians were entering it in force. The bootlegging of liquor and the operation of illicit drinking places (often in conjunction with gambling or prostitution) became big business—and a highly competitive business. The Italian gangsters had two decisive advantages in this violent and deadly competition: (1) *they could traffic in liquor without themselves becoming alcoholics*, and (2) *family loyalties were as central to Italian crime as to Italian life in general.* Sobriety and loyalty were particularly important in a life-and-death business" (*Ethnic America*, New York: Basic Books Inc., 1981, p. 125). (emphasis added)

The principle of using vice without becoming addicted to vice has proven invaluable to all of the dynastic families, even the families of the Mafia. The principle works because it is a corruption of an extremely important Biblical truth which wise Christian parents teach their children: *negotiating around vice without losing integrity*! We think of the spies who lodged in Rahab's household (Joshua 2). We think of Moses, who was in Pharaoh's household for 40 years.

During one of the worst times in the history of Israel, a wicked centralist king named Ahab was on the throne (1 Kings 16-21). God raised up two important Biblical leaders, one on the outside, Elijah, and one on the inside, Obadiah (1 Kings 18). Many Christians know about the great prophet Elijah who called down fire from heaven. Unfortunately, few have even heard about the inside man, Obadiah. He was second in command next to Ahab, so he had a very high and important advisory position with the King. Yet, all the time he was advising the King, he was able to hide out one hundred prophets in caves. He used his position under a statist King to hide the prophets, and did not become addicted to statism or Baalism.

The wise man who lives among unbelievers and their pagan ways is able to build the Kingdom of God by negotiating around vice without losing integrity. That's difficult and takes a mature man in Christ, but the great men and women of the Bible did this time and again. To be specific, it may even mean using vice without becoming involved in sin.

Pat Robertson's Original Strategy

A modern-day example is the story behind the rapid growth of Pat Robertson's television ministry. He wanted people to own satellite reception dishes to receive his broadcasts. People inside the cable TV industry believe that Robertson (a lawyer) guessed that the satellite dish industry could have been stopped short if the networks or the satellite networks had been able to persuade Congress to make private, home-owned satellite reception dishes illegal. So he devised an ingenious answer: he took the copyright off his broadcasts. Anyone can legally receive his network's satellite broadcasts. Had the owner been approached by some government bureaucrat and told to take down his dish, he could always say, "I bought it so that I can watch the 700 Club." Thus, the Federal Government would find it very difficult to block the sale and installation of reception dishes: "freedom of speech, freedom of religion."

There was another secret of his success. When local cable stations were beginning to start up, owners knew there would be howls of righteous protest against soft-core pornography and violence. R-rated movies were scheduled for broadcast by HBO and its competitors, and these would be the financial backbone of cable television's late-night programming. The cable operators needed a way to deflect criticism. Pat Robertson became every operator's excuse.

"Look," he could say to local regulators, "we offer a wide variety of programming. We have something for everyone. We have Christian programming, too." Guess *whose* Christian programming? The man who got there first. Pat Robertson, being a man of destiny and discipline, had seen the opportunity. Even though HBO was going to show unacceptable movies — movies that Robertson would not have allowed to be shown if he had possessed the power to stop them — he still offered his free programming to cable stations.

The result: every station that picked up HBO also broadcast the 700 Club to subscribers as a free bonus. Not only did that become the stepping stone to the broad popularity of the station, but many have been converted as a result. This is the kind of discipline that, coupled with destiny and dominion, builds dynasties.

We should understand, however, that the advent of sin into the world corrupted man's will to dominate. The cross of Christ, however, renewed not only the will but the ability to dominate. Regrettably, the modern Christian family has forgotten or hidden from what the unbeliever is self conscious about. The great dynastic families, without a shadow of a doubt, attempt to dominate. They see nothing wrong with dominion, with wanting dominion, with having dominion, with studying dominion principles, and consequently, they have the dominion.

For that matter, the basic patterns we have observed in mostly pagan family empires — destiny, discipline, and dominion — have been generally recognized by them. They may not call these principles by the same names, but the point is that pagan dynasties are self-conscious. The average Christian family is not even aware that God wants his family to grow and have great influence for *generations*. Not just one generation. Generational influence is powerful. The Christian family, therefore, fails by default.

Summary

I have tried to answer one basic question: Who owns the future generation?

1. I answered this question by beginning with the case involving the father of a girl who was already in the covenant. A minister wanted to re-baptize her. When this situation went to court, it was ruled that the girl was in the covenant already. This indicates a certain rationale.

2. I call it the generational principle. Children of believers are to be placed in the covenant and trained in the ways of the covenant. God owns the future through the principle of *generational expansion of the faith*. That's why the State tries to curb this kind of growth, any way it can. For this reason, we need to become self-conscious about building for the future through our children.

3. A covenantal dynasty. I pointed out three Biblical precepts involved in generational growth: destiny, discipline, and dominion. This world belongs to God's people. It will be here until all things are under the dominion of Christ. The way to arrive at *victory* is through the raising up of a "holy seed," from generation to generation.

This concludes our "ten principles." Now its time to apply this information and see what the family, Church, and State can do to put ownership back into the proper hands. Before we do that, however, I want to summarize in the next chapter what we have covered so far.

Can you name all ten principles? Can you remember some of the court cases? Can you recall the five-fold covenantal model? Let's turn to the following chapter, and *review* before we move on to the "applications" section.

CONCLUSION

Let's summarize what we've done so far. Do you remember the ten principles? Do you recall the ten cases and pieces of legislation? How about the title of the book? Can you call to mind what this book is all about?

The title of this book is *Who Owns the Family?* I've tried to answer this question by means of ten principles, all developed around ten pieces of legislation and/or cases that have changed family life in America.

Principle 1: the principle of *sacred covenant*. I started with "Covenant, not Contract?" Why? The place to begin in answering the question, "Who owns the family?" is here. In a famous case in 1888, *Maynard v. Hill*, it was established that the family is not a "mere contract," but a *sacred covenant*, an "institution."

I defined a sacred covenant as a "five-fold bond." Using the Book of Deuteronomy as a model, a marriage covenant consists of the following: *transcendence*, *hierarchy*, *ethics*, *sanctions*, and *continuity*, a "bond."

Using this basic grid, the outline of the principles themselves followed the five points of the covenant twice. So, the first chapter establishes that the family is created by God; it is *transcendent* because it is a *sacred covenant*; it, not the State, is the *trustee* of children.

Principle 2: the principle of *authority*. Chapter 2 is called "By Whose Authority?" Recent legislation, particularly *New Jersey v. T.L.O.*, encroaches on the family. In this particular case it was ruled that teachers are not surrogate parents. The case was used to limit the power of teachers to search, but in the process, the whole zone of education was taken from the parents.

120

The principle in this chapter is that God is the authority. Neither State nor family have final authority over the family. God does, and God entrusts the family with a "delegated authority."

Principle 3: the principle of law. The chapter is called "By What Standard?" I wanted to emphasize that the State does not determine the standard for the family. I used the famous, *Nebraska ex rel. Douglas v. Faith Baptist Church*. The issue was: "by what standard" will children of the Church be raised and educated? Faith Baptist Church argued that their standard was the Bible.

Since God has delegated His standard to the family, as well as to every sphere of society, I used the Ten Commandments as a guide, relating each commandment to show the ramifications of Biblical law.

Principle 4: the principle of *sanctions*. I referred to the amazing "Snyder Case" where parents tried to take their "incorrigible" daughter to the State for disciplinary help. Instead of helping them, the State bent the law to take their daughter away.

The Bible gives parents the authority to discipline. Sure, they can give an "incorrigible" teenager over for serious discipline. But the State has no right to take children from parents, unless the parents are genuinely "abusing" the child. So that Biblical discipline is understood, I presented Biblical methods of punishment.

Principle 5: the principle of *inheritance*. "Family Inheritance" was the title of this chapter. Here, I presented the damaging legislation of the 16th Amendment, the income tax law. Why was it so damaging? It was made a tax on *success*, the first "graduated tax" in our nation's history. This cut into the "inheritance" of families.

Why is inheritance important? It is a powerful tool for building up families over *generations*. Of course, inheritance is *intangible* (character traits, etc.) and *tangible*. If parents can pass on a spiritual and fiscal legacy, they are arming the next generation with an inheritance that can overcome the world, the flesh, and the Devil. In the last half of this chapter, using the inheritance passages of the Bible, I summarized some guidelines for parents to keep in mind.

Principle 6: the principle of *life*. "Who Owns Life?" was the name of this chapter. Keeping in mind the covenantal grid, I restated the five points of a *sacred covenant*. This parallels with the 6th of the Ten Commandments, "You shall not murder." The important legislation here is *Roe v. Wade*. For the first time, the State set itself up as the final determinant of life and death. The Bible says that this privilege belongs only to God. Since God considers *unborn babies* human beings, so should the State. The most serious problem with *Roe v. Wade* is that it destroyed the whole concept of "due process," the right of trial by jury.

Principle 7: the principle of *sexual privacy*. One case that I considered was *People v. Onofre*. The other was *Griswold v. Connecticut*. The issue was the "boundary of sexual privacy." The first case placed sexual privacy *outside of marriage*. All kinds of sexual perversity were allowed: homosexuality, lesbianism, etc.

Does this mean the Bible is against sex? No. God created man and woman, so He is not against sex. He's against sex *outside of marriage*. In the remainder of the chapter, I presented some basic principles for sex in marriage.

Principle 8: the principle of *worldview*. The title of the chapter is "Whose Worldview?" I wanted to discuss the whole question of education. But, the real issue at risk is *worldview*. In *Ohio v. Whisner* it was established that education determines a child's entire worldview, which makes education a *religious question*. Evidently the State saw this because it said, "The real question is not which religion is the best religion, but how shall the best be secured."

What is the correct worldview? Using the "covenantal grid" of the first chapter, I briefly developed a *covenantal worldview*.

Principle 9: the principle of *protection*. This chapter was called "Who Protects the Family, and How?" I used the famous *Quinlan Case* to demonstrate that the family needs other *institutional protection*. The State protects the family by implementing the capital offense laws of the Bible, seeing all of these crimes are directly against the family. The Church, however, protects the family by being a true *guardian* of the needs of the family. The Church and not the State is given this responsibility.

Principle 10: the principle of *generational growth*. The final principle is called "Who Owns the Future Generation?" It's about the *generational expansion of Christianity*. In a famous case involving a Mr. Armstrong (1842), a minister tried to *re-baptize* his daughter, after she had already been baptized. The court ruled the minister was "out of line," interfering with the covenantal obligations of Mr. Armstrong as father. The Biblical basis for this ruling was even included in the judge's remarks. Why? Scripture teaches that children are part of the covenant, and to be claimed by God.

In this chapter, I included three basic guidelines for rearing a Christian dynasty: Destiny, Discipline, Dominion.

This is a future orientation of the family. God entrusts it to the parents.

Summary

So, I've presented the ten principles of family ownership. This chapter has attempted to provide a brief summary.

But, the task is not complete. We still need to *apply* what we've learned about the family. By way of application, I want to discuss what the family, church, and state can do to put the trusteeship of the family back into the parents' hands. In the following chapter, I want to begin with the family.

What can the family do? Is it helpless? Are there specific things your family can be doing? Yes. Let's turn to the next chapter to find out!

Part II
RECONSTRUCTION

11

WHAT CAN THE FAMILY DO?

In the "Introduction," I said there are two parts to this book: principles and application. The principles section answers the question, "Who owns the family?" Let's not misunderstand each other, even at this late point in the book. *God owns the family.* Every family. He has entrusted it with several sacred obligations. So, using the covenant model presented in the first chapter, I have covered ten critical areas where proper trusteeship has been given by God, and where the State has tried to take the Lord's good gifts from the family.

Now we should turn to some practical questions. "Fine," you may be saying, "I accept these principles, but after all, aren't we starting a little late in the game? What can *my* family do to put ownership of the family back in the proper hands?"

Excellent question. I've been asking it myself concerning my family, too. In the last three chapters of this book, I want to talk about *how ownership of the family is put back into the hands of the proper trustees*!

First, I want to tell you *what your family can do.*

Second, I would like to instruct you *what your church can do.*

Third, finally I need to lay out a plan as to *what the State can do.*

You're absolutely right if you're thinking, "It's late in the game." But it's *never too late.* God is on *our side*, and that's all that matters.

Fallen Christian cultures have turned around before. Take the 1700s in England, for example. England had become very decadent. The Church was weak. The family was even weaker, and

Christians were beginning to wonder what would happen to this once great Christian nation.

God's people rolled up their sleeves and got busy reclaiming a nation that belonged to God. They called on Him to honor His Word, as He had promised in His Word:

> When I shut up heaven and there is no rain, or command the locusts to devour the land, or send pestilence among My people, if My people who are called by My name will humble themselves, and pray and seek My face, and turn from their wicked ways, then I will hear from heaven, and will forgive their sin and heal their land (II Chronicles 7:13-14).

England recaptured its Christian heritage through the great preaching of George Whitfield and John Wesley. Wesley's preaching literally sobered up hundreds of thousands of the English working class. It made them thrifty, future-oriented people. His message of eternal salvation and earthly responsibility laid the groundwork of the Industrial Revolution, which began in the 1780s.

Contrast England to France. The French were also a people who had once been faithful to God, but had turned away from their covenant. Did they come back to the Lord? No. Instead their leaders listened to the *philosophes*, a group of pagan, God-hating philosophers who thought the future hope of France was in an evolutionary and revolutionary view of man, and not God.

The histories of England and France are quite different from that point on. From 1789 to 1795, France went through a bloody revolution. By the end of the 1790s, Napoleon Bonaparte, a ruthless military dictator, had come to power. He marched France into military victories, and then defeat. French political life was disrupted by the Revolution, and it has never fully recovered. Political instability coupled with stagnant bureaucracy have been the marks of French life for almost two centuries.

England, on the other hand, sailed into one of its finest hours from the 1780s onward. England's share of world trade soared; she became the master of the seas. Industrial production increased rapidly with the Industrial Revolution. By 1850, England was the richest nation on earth, an honor France had held eighty years earlier. There were still problems, but nothing compared to France's problems.

America is today at the same crossroads. It can go the way of nineteenth-century England, or decline like France.

We should remember, however, that it is late; we should not waste any of our efforts. The "Christian capital" of our forefathers is just about used up. We need to remember the words of Hezekiah, an ancient king of Israel who came to power when Israel was in sin. God convicted him and this is what he said in an address to the nation.

Children of Israel, return to the Lord God of Abraham, Isaac, and Israel; then He will return to the remnant of you who have escaped from the hand of the kings of Assyria. And do not be like your fathers and your brethren, who trespassed against the Lord God of their fathers, so that He gave them up to astonishment, as you see. Now do not be stiff-necked, as your fathers were, but yield yourselves to the Lord; and enter His sanctuary, which He has sanctified forever, and serve the Lord your God, that the fierceness of His wrath may turn away from you. If you return to the Lord, your brethren and your children will be treated with compassion by those who lead them captive, so that they may come back to this land; for the Lord your God is gracious and merciful, and will not turn His face from you if you return to Him (II Chronicles 30:6-9).

Wouldn't it be great if the President of the United States gave a speech like Hezekiah's? *The same words apply to God's people today!* Paul says the Church is the new Israel of God when he says to the *Church at Galatia*, "And as many as walk according to this rule, peace and mercy be upon them, and upon the *Israel of God*" (Galatians 6:16). (emphasis added)

America was claimed long ago by the Church of Jesus Christ. Our presidents are sworn in with their hands on an open Bible. They take their *oath of office* with a commitment to the Christian faith. Sure, a lot of them did not honor their vow, but God took what they did seriously. So, America has been pledged to Christ.

She is obligated to come back to the Lord, just like Israel of old.

Let's begin with the *family*. Returning ownership of the family to the proper trustees will have to be part of America's return to Christ. In this chapter, I want to present three things *you can do with your family* to put its ownership back into the right hands.

Church Membership

The first thing you need to do with your family is *join a good Church*, and submit your family to the discipline of *worship*. Remember the passage I mentioned earlier about King Hezekiah? Listen to what the people did after hearing they needed to return to God's House.

> Now many people, a very great congregation, assembled at Jerusalem to keep the Feast of Unleavened Bread in the second month. They arose and took away the altars that were in Jerusalem, and they took away all the incense altars and cast them into the Brook Kidron. Then they slaughtered the Passover lambs on the fourteenth day of the second month. The priests and the Levites were ashamed, and sanctified themselves, and brought the burnt offerings to the house of the Lord. They stood in their place according to their custom, according to the Law of Moses the man of God; the priests sprinkled blood which they received from the hand of the Levites. For there were many in the congregation who had not sanctified themselves; therefore the Levites had charge of the slaughter of the Passover lambs for everyone who was not clean, to sanctify them to the Lord. For a multitude of the people, many from Ephraim, Manasseh, Issachar, and Zebulun, had not cleansed themselves, yet they ate the Passover contrary to what was written. But Hezekiah prayed for them saying, "May the good Lord provide atonement for everyone who prepares his heart to seek God, the Lord God of his fathers, though he is not cleansed according to the purification of the sanctuary." And the Lord listened to Hezekiah and healed the people. . . . The whole congregation of Judah rejoiced, also the priest and the Levites, all the congregation that came from Israel, the sojourners who came from the land of Israel, and those who dwelt in Judah. So there was great joy in Jerusalem. . . . Then the priests, the Levites, arose

and blessed the people, and their voice was heard; and their prayer came up to His holy dwelling place, to heaven. Now when all this was finished, all Israel who were present went out to the cities of Judah and *broke the sacred (pagan) pillars in pieces, cut down the wooden images, and threw down the high places and the altars*—from Judah, Benjamin, Ephraim, and Manasseh—until they had utterly destroyed them all. Then all the children of Israel returned to their own cities, *every man to his possessions* (II Chronicles 30:13-31:1). (emphasis added)

Hezekiah told the people they needed to return. Where did they begin? Worship. Where did they end? "Every man returned to his *possessions*." In other words, ownership went back to the proper trustees of the family. Is this what you want? Then the place to begin is around God's throne.

The Bible begins here. Earlier, I talked about how Christ restored the family. The principle I emphasized was, *"Honor God's family, and He'll honor yours."*

You want to know why family life has degenerated in America? It is because families have turned away from the Lord. If they don't honor God, then He will not honor them.

Look at all the efforts to save the family: Presidential commissions, millions of books, magazine articles, psychological studies, and even television shows. How many of them ever mention the *Church* and *worship before God's throne*? None!

In the late 1940s, there was a radio program called (if memory serves me correctly) the "Family Hour." (Naturally, it lasted only a half hour.) It ended each show with this slogan: "The family that prays together stays together." The place to begin is the *Church*, around God's throne, worship, and God's house.

What Should You Look For in a Church?

1. You want to find a church that believes in the Word of God. How can you tell? Here are a list of questions you can ask to find out what the church believes. Ask the pastor and the officers.

- Does the church believe in a 24-hour, six-day creation?
- Does the church believe in all sixty-six books, historically accurate — literal creation, Fall of Adam and Eve, Jonah in the belly of a whale, etc. — *inerrant* Word of God?
- Does the church believe in the Holy Trinity? One God in three persons. Does it believe all three persons are eternally existent God?
- Does the church believe Jesus really died and rose again in three days?
- Does the church believe Jesus ascended bodily to heaven and now sits at the right hand of God?
- Does the church believe in one baptism and Holy Communion?
- Does the church believe the Church is bigger than its own denomination or local church?
- Does the church believe a Christian is supposed to obey the Ten Commandments, with the only exception being that the Sabbath (the fourth commandment) is now on Sunday, and no longer on Saturday, because this was the day Christ was resurrected?
- Does the church believe and pray the Lord's prayer (Matthew 6:9-13)?
- Does the church believe that Jesus will come again and judge the world for all its sin?
- Does the church believe its members are supposed to believe all the doctrines covered in these questions?

If a church does not believe these things, then find one that does. Remember, ideas have consequences. You may think you can attend a church and ignore the theology. You may think the preaching won't affect you and your family. You may think "nonsexist" liturgy can't hurt anyone. Think again.

I knew a conservative man who would not leave his liberal church. He was quite wealthy and his family had personally contributed thousands, maybe even several million to the denomination. He wouldn't leave. First, his church allowed men in the pulpit who didn't believe in the inerrancy of the Bible. Second, his church allowed women's ordination. Third, ordination of homosexuals. Fourth, prayers to father/mother God.

All this time he thought he could fend off the effects of the bad theology. For years he watched his children grow-up in his large, beautiful, but liberal church. Sadly, one by one his children turned out to be *second-generation socialists*. He had had the strength to fight the bad theology—or had he, seeing what he had done to his family—but the children couldn't.

He lost them all. Sure his church had a lot of youth, money, beauty, choirs, nice services, ladies' and mens' groups, etc., etc. But what was it all worth in the final analysis? Nothing. So find a church that believes the right things.

2. The second thing you want to look for in a church is sound *practice*. There are two criteria: Christian education and pro-life emphasis. If a church does not have these and is not at least working toward them, forget it. There is no neutrality. You can't afford to have your family in a church that is anti-Christian education and pro-death.

Are the church's leaders sending their own children to Christian schools? If not, don't join unless there is no other alternative in town. (And maybe you should consider moving.) The church's leadership is weak.

Are the church's leaders actively opposing abortion? Do they picket the local abortion mill regularly? If not, don't join unless there is no other alternative in town. (And maybe you should consider moving.) The church's leadership is weak.

So, the first thing you need to do with your family is find a good church, become a part of it, tithe your money to the Lord through it, and support it in every way. Remember what we learned about the Karen Ann Quinlan case? The individual is not enough. It will take a strong Church to offset statist trends. If you want ownership of the family to return to God's trustees, the Church is the place to begin.

Christian Education

The second most important thing you and your family can do is get involved in the *Christian school movement*. From a pragmatic point of view, consider how much time a school-age child spends with his teachers. If teachers are not committed to Christianity, they will probably have more influence over the child. As the Roman Catholic Church used to say, "Give us a child until he's 9-years-old, and he'll probably always be a Catholic." That's why, no doubt, after Biblical worship, Christian education has done more, and will do more, to change the nation than anything else. The Christian education movement has done two things to change our world.

Creationism

Are you aware that for well over 100 years evolutionary ideas have bombarded Christian civilization? For the most part, Christianity has been losing. It was not until the creation movement was picked up by the independent Christian school movement that the situation began to change in our culture.

Evolution says that the material world is eternal, making "God" part of the evolutionary development of creation, not the Creator.

So what? So everything! This ancient pagan concept has been resurrected to affect every area of thought. If the world was created by God, then matter is not eternal; there is one true God; there is an absolute standard. If men don't believe in Him, then what He says will happen, will happen.

If, on the other hand, there is not a definite Creator, then there is no absolute truth. Everything is in process. All process theology is evolutionistic and relativistic.

Starting with religion, say the process theologians, there is not one correct religion because according to evolution, man started out believing in many gods (polytheism) and evolved into the belief in one God. Christianity teaches that man started out believing in one God, and devolved after the Fall to believe in many gods.

> For the wrath of God is revealed from heaven against all ungodliness and unrighteousness of men, who suppress the truth in unrighteousness, because what may be known of God is manifest in them, for God has shown it to them. For since the creation of the world His invisible attributes are clearly seen, being un-

derstood by things that are made, even His eternal power and Godhead, so that they are without excuse, because, although they knew God, they did not glorify Him as God, nor were thankful, but became futile in their thoughts, and their foolish hearts were darkened. Professing to be wise, they became fools, and changed the glory of the incorruptible God into an image made like corruptible man—and birds and four-footed beasts and creeping things (Romans 1:18-23).

The difference between the creationist and evolutionist emerges in every academic discipline, since man is a religious creature. In economics, there is no set, definite standard for how an economy is to be run. In law, there is no fixed law to which man is answerable, transcending above his national constitutions, or his interpretations.

Do you begin to get the picture? Creationism is at the center of the battle for our whole culture. With it comes the true belief that there is only one way to God and one standard, Christianity. That's why Christian schools play such an important role in putting the family back into the hands of the proper trustees.

If a Christian school "saves money" by using "free" state-approved textbooks, find another school. There's no sense in paying tuition to get warmed-over humanism with a morning prayer. Those prayers are just too expensive.

Moral Environment

The second effect of Christian education has been the creation of a better moral environment for children. A recent study revealed that if a child spends 40 or more hours a week in a day-care center, he will be permanently damaged psychologically. Why?

It's the *moral environment*. In many Christian circles, environment has been greatly *underestimated*. Solomon didn't underestimate it. Listen to what he tells fathers to teach their sons at the very beginning of his book.

My son, if sinners entice you, do not consent. If they say, "Come with us, let us lie in wait to shed blood; let us lurk secretly for the innocent without cause; let us swallow them alive like

Sheol, and whole, like those who go down to the Pit; we shall find all kinds of precious possessions, we shall fill our houses with spoil; cast in your lot among us, let us all have one purse"—My son, do not walk in the way with them, keep your foot from their path; for their feet run to evil, and they make haste to shed blood. Surely, in vain the net is spread in the sight of any bird; but they lie in wait for their own blood, they lurk secretly for their own lives. So are the ways of everyone who is greedy for gain; it takes away life of its owners (Proverbs 1:10-19).

Why do you think Solomon begins the most practical book on wisdom in the Bible with a section on *staying away from the wrong kind of company*? Environment is probably the single most important principle for becoming a wise man. Haven't you heard the saying that great men are usually found in groups of other great men? It's true. It's just as true that a good moral environment is what Christian parents are really paying for.

I know Christian parents who send their children to public schools because the parents think (or at least they *say* they think) that public schools provide a better education. They define education as *morally neutral technical skills*, and they accept the public school as a *morally neutral environment.*

After all, there hasn't been a drug bust in the local high school for over a month. Not one gang confrontation this semester. And the fact that Planned Parenthood has just set up an advisory service on campus is irrelevant, even if they do tell the girls where to get contraceptives and abortions without parental knowledge or consent. Other than that, everything is squeaky clean morally.

But in 1958, parents would have recalled the school board, fired the principal, and called in the police. The "horrors" Glenn Ford confronted in the "Blackboard Jungle" back in 1954 are alive and well in the suburbs. Nobody was on drugs in "Blackboard Jungle." Planned Parenthood didn't exist in 1954.

Christian Hypocrisy

Ask such parents why they send their children to church or Sunday school. "Why, to get a good foundation in morality!" For two whole hours a week. Question: Why do the children need a moral foundation? "To protect them from today's immoral environment!" Question: Just what immoral environment are they in? Silence. Angry silence. You have just blown their cover. You have just confronted them with their own hypocrisy.

The children have been sent by their parents into the most immoral environment they are likely ever to face as Americans (unless we suffer a military defeat), the most consistently anti-Christian environment in America: the public school system.

They may blurt out, "We want the best education possible for our kids." Horsefeathers. For a generation, national test scores of graduating seniors have been declining. Test scores of students in Christian schools are consistently above grade level. Everyone knows this, especially the parents who refuse to act in terms of this knowledge.

But even if the public schools did prepare children better to take tests prepared by public school educators, it would be irrelevant. Christian philosopher Cornelius Van Til has said it best: "It doesn't matter how well you sharpen a saw that's set off angle; it will never cut straight. Sharpen it, and it will still cut crooked, only faster." No matter how technically competent the local public high school is—and declining test scores for a generation indicate that it isn't competent at all—the question isn't technical competence; the questions are *religious presuppositions* and *moral environment*.

We shouldn't be misled. Christian parents know what they're doing when they send their children into the public schools. They know that the public schools are Baal-worshipping moral cesspools. The fundamental issue is that *they're too cheap to pay the Christian school's tuition*. All the baloney about religiously neutral textbooks and a neutral moral environment is nonsense, and they know it. There is no neutrality in the war between good and evil, between Christ and Satan, and every Christian knows it. Some just won't admit it when there's money involved.

Maybe, just maybe, it isn't a question of money. Maybe it's that Dad wants Junior to be captain of the football team someday, or Mom wants Sis to be homecoming queen. Maybe the local Christian school doesn't have a football team or a homecoming prom. Such parents have twisted, anti-Christian priorities, and they are willing to sacrifice their children's moral, intellectual, and even physical safety on the altar of vicarious adult thrills.

A Challenge to Humanist Civilization

So, creationism and a moral environment are the two great forces of Christian education. These have been unleashed on humanist society, and are also challenging a stagnant, compromising brand of Christianity that is all the last generation knew.

Let's face it, we're just beginning a new program of cultural renewal with our generation. Most of us, and most of the people who read this book, will be first-generation Christians who were educated in public schools. Our children will be the ones to begin to see the true resurgence of Christianity and its cultural effects.

But we have to begin right now! If we're going to return to the family what God has given it, we will have to put our children in Christian schools, and join the fight. There are two options: Christian schools and home-schooling. My purpose is not to debate the two in this book. Both are important and both are valid.

It's the validity of both that singles out the issue. *Parents, not the State, have the responsibility of choosing what method of education they'll use.* Not the State. As long as we allow the State to take our children, while we have little time to put them in Christian schools, we are more likely to lose the battle. But if we take advantage now, and pay the price, even a double price for this generation (taxes and tuition), we can win back ownership for the family in the future.

Christian Activism

The third thing you and your family can do is become *Christian activists*. I didn't say revolutionaries. What's the difference?

A revolutionary acts outside the law: he blows up buildings, steals, kidnaps businessmen, counterfeits money, etc.

A Christian activist acts within the law: he writes his congressman, pays his taxes while opposing taxation that is more than the tithe to God's house, pickets abortion clinics, works in Christian school efforts, etc.

A Christian activist acts lawfully to create a Christian culture. He does concrete, roll-up-the-shirtsleeves types of things.

But some Christians think this is too much. In the town where I live, there are a bunch of Christians who think it is wrong to picket an abortion clinic. They say, "We should just pray and leave the rest to God."

Is this right?

No. Prayer is where you start. Prayer is where you finish. It's in between prayers that we're arguing about.

Did you know there is a time when prayer isn't enough? Listen to the words of Isaiah.

> Hear the word of the Lord, you rulers of Sodom; give ear to the law of our God, you people of Gomorrah: "To what purpose is the multitude of your sacrifices to Me?" Says the Lord. "I have had enough of burnt offerings of rams and the fat of fed cattle. I do not delight in the blood of bulls, or of lambs or goats. When you come to appear before Me, who has required this from your hand, to trample My courts? Bring no more futile sacrifices; Incense is an abomination to Me. The New Moons and your appointed feasts My soul hates; They are a trouble to Me, I am weary of bearing them. When you spread out your hands, I will hide My eyes from you; even though *you make many prayers*, *I will not hear.* Your hands are full of blood. Wash yourselves, make yourselves clean; Put away the evil of your doings from before My eyes. Cease to do evil, learn to do good; seek justice, reprove the oppressor; defend the fatherless, plead for the widow. Come now, and let us reason together." Says the Lord. "Though your sins are like scarlet, they shall be as white as snow; though they are red like crimson, they shall be as wool. If you are willing and obedient, you shall eat the good of the land; but if you refuse and rebel, you shall be devoured by the sword"; for the mouth of the Lord has spoken (Isaiah 1:10-20).

Prayer is not enough! I know that may sound terribly "unspiritual" in days like ours, but it's true. Prayer is not enough! It never was.

God expects us to be publicly active for our faith. Have you ever considered that more people in America belong to the "institutional" Church than any other organization? That's right. What would happen if Christians really stood up and were counted?

What if they went into the voting booth, and had their ballots counted? What if they simply voted "no" on every school bond election?

Just the few Christians who have stood up have sent political shockwaves through the ranks of liberal humanists. For example, for the last 50 years, political liberals have used ministers and religious people to rally their cause. "Christians have a moral responsibility to come out of their closets and get involved politically," the National Council of Churches preached for half a century. All right, they have finally come out. Now the National Council-types are horrified. Listen to the liberal hue and cry against "fundamentalists" getting involved in politics. It's all a bunch of hypocrisy.

Christians *are* supposed to be involved in everything because they're the only·ones with the right answers. Bible-based answers. Anti-National Council of Churches-type answers.

When the liberals scream, tough bananas. Christian involvement is what we're supposed to do. That's what *you're supposed to do*. That's what millions of Christians are beginning to do. That's what a lot more are going to do. The battle is just beginning. But *you* have to begin now. It's not so much a matter of "what" you do, as long as it's lawful. *Just do something*!

Become a Christian activist and model commitment before your children. When I was learning to be a teacher, they used to tell me that people retain a lot more if they see, hear, and *do* what is taught. You have many opportunities to teach your children how to be *dedicated Christians*. As James says,

> But be *doers* of the word, and not hearers only, deceiving yourselves. For if anyone is a hearer of the word and not a *doer*, he is like a man observing his natural face in a mirror; for he observes himself, goes away, and immediately forgets what kind of man he was. But he who looks into the perfect law of liberty and continues

in it, and is not a forgetful hearer but a doer of the word, this one will be blessed in what he does (James 1:22-25). (emphasis added)

Summary

Can you remember this chapter's title? Can you remember the three things you should do if you want to help put the family back into the hands of its proper trustees?

The title of the chapter is "What Can the Family Do?" It's the first of three chapters on the application of all that we have learned from the ten principles in the first part of the book.

The three things that a family can do are: (1) join a good Church and become faithful, (2) get involved in the Christian school movement, and (3) become a Christian activist.

12

WHAT CAN THE CHURCH DO?

We often forget the Church can do something. That's not
meant entirely as a criticism. We've seen so many churches go liberal and become irrelevant. Or, maybe we haven't seen any that
do much of anything. Think for a moment. How many churches
in your community take a stand *as a church*? Not many, I'll bet. I
know that in my town the largest churches are usually the most
compromised. They won't take a position on abortion. They won't
get involved in the Christian education battle.

But maybe we don't consider the Church because we're so
used to thinking in terms of *individuals*. Do you know of any books
or tapes that talk about "how the institutional Church can change
society"? How ironic. Americans are an extremely religious people. I've already pointed out that the Church is the single largest
organization (however fragmented) in America. At a number of
places, I've even suggested that the Church can do *more* than an
individual.

Why is this? Hear the words of Christ.

> I also say to you that you are Peter, and on this rock I will build
> My church, and the gates of Hades shall not prevail against it.
> And I will give you the keys of the kingdom of heaven, and what-
> ever you bind on earth will be bound in heaven, and whatever you
> loose on earth will be loosed in heaven (Matthew 16:18-19).

He didn't say He would build His political party, His family,
His Christian school system, His tract society, His satellite radio
network, or His corporation. He said, "I will build my *church*."
Hades will not be taken by the Society of Christian Joggers,

142

Christian publishers, or Christian movie producers.

We should keep in mind that Christ is talking about the Church as an *institution*, not a bunch of individuals floating around. Hell will not prevail against the institutional Church. The fact is that many individuals will fall, but not the Church as the Church.

Having said this, let's put the words about "binding and loosing" in "the institutional Church context." Individuals don't bind and loose. The Church does. An individual may act on behalf of the Church, but that's the point. He's not doing it, or should not be doing it, as an individual. It's the Church that will overpower the kingdom of darkness.

How?

Christ destroys hell with "keys." Immediately after Christ promises that hell can't stand against the Church, He tells Peter that he has been given "keys" to "bind and loose." What do "keys" do? They open and shut doors. So, by the "mere" power of opening and shutting the door of the kingdom of heaven, *hell is destroyed*.

What are these keys? There are three things that open and shut the door of the kingdom of heaven.

One, *preaching* of the Word of God opens and shuts the door. Paul says,

> How then shall they call on Him in whom they have not believed? And how shall they believe in Him of whom they have not heard? And how shall they hear without a preacher? And how shall they preach unless they are sent? As it is written: How beautiful are the feet of those who preach the gospel of peace who bring glad tidings of good things (Romans 10:14-15).

Two, the *sacraments* of baptism and communion open and shut the door. Communion, for example, can serve the function of *shutting* the door. Paul says,

> Therefore whoever eats this bread or drinks this cup of the Lord in an unworthy manner will be guilty of the body and blood of the Lord. But let a man examine himself, and so let him eat of that bread and drink of that cup. For he who eats and drinks in an

unworthy manner, *eats and drinks judgment to himself*, not discerning the Lord's body. For this reason many are *weak and sick among you, and many sleep*. For if we would judge ourselves, we would not be judged. But when we are judged, we are chastened by the Lord, that we may not be condemned with the world (I Corinthians 11:27-32).

Three, *discipline* opens and shuts the door to the kingdom. It can open the door in that it retrieves a wayward brother. James says, "Brethren, if anyone among you wanders from the truth, and someone turns him back, let him know that he who turns a sinner from the error of his way will save a soul from death and cover a multitude of sins" (James 5:19-20).

Discipline can also shut the door in an attempt to restore. Paul says:

> It is actually reported that there is sexual immorality among you, and such sexual immorality as is not even named among the Gentiles — that a man has his father's wife! . . . deliver such a one to Satan for the destruction of the flesh, that his spirit may be saved in the day of the Lord Jesus" (I Corinthians 5:1-5).

So, the Church, and the Church alone, is given the power of the "keys." With preaching, the sacraments, and discipline, it destroys hell.

The program for returning ownership of the family back to the rightful trustees, therefore, turns on these three "keys." If the Church is going to affect the State, it's going to have to use these "keys." There's simply no other Biblical way. In the following, I would like to outline several things in each area that would change the Church, and consequently change society. That is, if we are to believe that it is the institutional Church that destroys hell, then the change will have to come from the "keys" given to it. Here is *what the Church can do*.

True Prophetic Preaching

Too often, prophecy is viewed only as "telling something that will happen in the future." Certainly this is one aspect. But, telling what will happen should be kept in the proper context. The "forth-telling" is always in a *judicial setting*. It announces judgment.

When Jonah went to Nineveh, for example, he told them what would happen if they did not repent. Here is what he said,

"Yet forty days and Nineveh will be overthrown" (Jonah 3:4). What did he mean? Jonah told them that God was going to judge them for their sins *if* they did not repent. This is what we lack in our culture.

Soft-Core Salvation

A few weeks ago, I saw one of the nation's leading evangelists on a television talk show. The interviewer was definitely not a Christian. He came right out and asked the evangelist if he thought that AIDS is a judgment sent by God. The evangelist said, "No, God wouldn't do such a thing."

Odd, isn't it? This evangelist believes that God will send millions and perhaps even billions of people to hell for all eternity, to be forced to tolerate screaming intolerable agony and loneliness forever, without hope forever. But God wouldn't send a few thousand homosexual perverts the plague of AIDS as a warning to them and others of judgment to come.

Compared to hell, AIDS is nickel and dime sort of judgment. But the evangelist is afraid to admit in public that God judges sinners *in history* as a down payment on future eternal judgment, or to warn them about the coming eternal judgment. God's judgments are somehow outside of history. It's pie in the sky by and by, and it's boil in the oil in the soil.

But for the present, judgment is all very distant. Why, AIDS is no more a judgment of God than, say, herpes.

With respect to his doctrine of history, our evangelist is a liberal, and a wimpy liberal at that. Liberals don't want God's judgment in history, either. Such judgment points to hell, and this is *the* offending doctrine for liberals. Also for atheists.

History belongs to man.

In our society, there is usually no connection between what happens in the world and God's law. This vital cause/effect relationship has been lost. Consequently, the concept of judgment has been lost.

Sure, there is a place to preach the love of God. But someone cannot understand the love of God until he knows about hell and judgment. It's like knowing about cleanliness without a doctrine of dirt. It's only when men understand what they have been delivered from that they begin to see the great love of God in Christ through His horrible death on the Cross.

The Church fails to condemn anything! No one wants to be thought of as "negative." The theory is that we already do live in a negative society. To tell people about negative things like judgment compounds the problem. Whose problem? The media-certified, respectability-seeking Christian.

It's good that medical doctors don't treat the diseases they deal with this way. A while back, I burned my leg in a grease fire. When I went in to see the doctor, he said that it was a bad burn, and I would have to have special therapy. The treatment was the most painful experience of my life. They had to scrape the dead skin away every other day. I needed "to take my medicine," as the saying goes, and I needed for my doctor to tell me exactly *what I needed*, whether I liked it or not. If he hadn't, I would have lost my leg.

And that was just a grease fire. It only affected my leg.

The Church is in a similar position. Only, it speaks to a society that is on fire with the judgment of God, a society that is eaten up with sin. There can be no soft message. It has to be hard, because we live in a hard society.

The message of Christ is wonderful. It is the answer for our dying world. But it is part of the Church's job to warn society, like Jonah, that it will be judged if it doesn't repent. The cause/effect relationship should be pointed out. Man sins, and judgment comes. It's that simple.

What preachers want today is to be left alone to preach soft-core salvation. Hard-core salvation implies hard-core judgment.

So, is AIDS a direct judgment of God? You bet. Is there any hope? An answer? Certainly. The Gospel is the "good news that

Christ has died for sin and has overcome the judgment of God through His Resurrection." And, the Resurrection can bring physical healing; It can even bring it to AIDS victims. There's a way out.

Institutionally, the medical experts say there is only one way out: *monogamy.* One man, one woman: permanently, till death (not from AIDS) do they part. The Church refuses to speak with as clear a voice as the medical experts.

What will it take to get the Church to speak with a clear voice? An outbreak of AIDS?

What will it take to get Christian parents to pull their children out of the public schools? An outbreak of AIDS? (I can hear the excuses: "Look, there hasn't been a reported case of AIDS on campus in over a month. And besides, our Charlie is making straight-A's." Sorry, Charlie.

The Church will have to start by telling the world that sin is the issue. America is in great sin. The State is in great sin. The Church is in great sin. Family life is in great sin. And, *it will all be destroyed through disease, war, and any number of appropriate methods if repentance does not come.*

If the Church proclaims this message, society will change. As far as I'm concerned, it's as though God is sending these judgments and waiting for His Church to speak. If it does, people will once again begin to listen. The State will listen. The family will get its trusteeship back.

Sacraments

The second thing the Church needs to do is take the sacraments seriously. Why do I imply that it doesn't?

Most churches only take communion four times a year. Scripture indicates that it should be taken often. When Paul went to Troas, Luke tells us, "Now on the *first day of the week*, when the disciples came together to *break bread*, Paul ready to depart the next day, spoke to them and continued the message until midnight" (Acts 20:7). The New Testament Church had communion *every week.*

But what does communion have to do with how the Church affects the world? Remember what Paul told the Corinthians? He said that communion provides a context for the Church to judge itself that it might not be "condemned with the world" (1 Corinthians 11:32).

When the Church takes communion and it is in sin, then its members are sickly and they die. That's what the Bible says. "For this reason many are weak and sick among you, and some sleep" (1 Corinthians 11:30). What this really means is that sinfulness brings judgment from the world. To be judged "with" the world means inevitably to be judged "by" the world. Therefore, I have to conclude that the opposition of the State is directly related to *sin in the Church*.

That's right. If the Church had its affairs in order, the State would change. But God deals with corruption in the Church by sending outside opposition and persecution. This is one of His tried and true methods for dealing with "sin in the camp." When Israel entered the Promised Land and conquered Jericho, it was told not to take anything from the city. One man, named Achan, disobeyed. Israel could not win a battle until *Achan was dealt with* (Joshua 7).

All through Israel's history we see the same thing. Eventually, God brings the Assyrians and Babylonians, tyrannical states, down on the Israelites because of *sin in the camp*. When we come to the New Testament, a story to which I've already referred leaps off the page: the account of Ananias and Sapphira (Acts 5:1ff.). In the same chapter, Luke records how the Church was meeting much opposition. Again, the principle being that when there is "sin in the camp," the Church is persecuted.

What does communion have to do with all of this? Communion is just that, communion with Christ. When the Church communes properly with Him, it is not *condemned with and therefore by the world*. But until the Church gets back to weekly communion, it will not have the opportunity to see all of its sin for what it is. Until it sees its sin for what it is, it cannot adequately deal with it, that is, purge it and get rid of it.

But the week your church restores weekly communion, watch out. Communion requires self-judgment. Weekly communion requires weekly self-judgment. Those whose sins condemn them are flushed out, and usually quite rapidly. The pressure of self-judgment is like popping a boil: if it isn't removed first by internal healing, it will make a mess when it lets loose. The church that doesn't stand ready to excommunicate, and do it systematically, will be torn apart by the effects of weekly communion.

No, this isn't true of long-dead liberal churches. Weekly communion doesn't bother them. All the people inside are spiritually weak or sleeping, so God doesn't bother with them any more. They don't suffer explosions; they just fade away.

Healing

Paul makes one other important connection to communion. Healing! How so?

Paul says, "For this reason many are weak and sick among you, and many sleep" (I Corinthians 11:30). Health is tied to the sacrament. Therefore, weekly communion leads to a healing ministry for the Church.

How important is a healing ministry? We can learn from our Charismatic brethren on this point. Healing is tied to sacramental communion with Christ. The Church's message ought to be that there is healing in communion with Jesus. Of course, this is not true in every case because sin is still present in the world. But certainly Paul makes this kind of connection to the Corinthian Church.

So does James. He says, "Is anyone among you sick? Let him call for the elders of the church, and let them pray over him, anointing him with oil in the name of the Lord. And the prayer of faith will save the sick, and the Lord will raise him up. And if he has committed sins, he will be forgiven. Confess your trespasses to one another, and pray for one another, that you may be healed" (James 5:14-16).

James emphasizes dealing properly with sin, just the way Paul did. Healing is part of a vital ministry of the Church, connected to communion with Christ.

But how does healing affect the rest of society? Show me a Church that heals the sick, and you'll find an influential Church in society. Let's face it. If the Church healed people, then society would come to its side. So would the State.

In the Roman Empire, there was a bishop sent to a certain town. He was bitterly opposed by the town's officials. One day a plague hit the community. A city official's daughter got the disease. He had heard that this bishop could heal, so he brought his daughter to the Church. By the grace of God, the girl was healed. Guess what happened? Virtually the whole town converted!

So, the second thing the Church can do to change society and put trusteeship of the family back into the hands of parents is to implement *weekly communion*.

Discipline

Third, the church can change society through *discipline*. What does church discipline have to do with changing the State? Paul gives the answer.

> Dare any of you, having a matter against another, go to law before the unrighteous, and not *before the saints*? Do you not know that the saints will judge the world? And if the world will be judged by you, are you unworthy to judge the smallest matters? Do you not know that we shall judge angels? How much more, things that pertain to this life? If then you have judgments concerning things pertaining to this life, do you appoint those who are least esteemed by the church to judge? I say this to your shame. Is it so, that there is not a wise man among you, not even one, who will be able to judge between his brethren? But brother goes to law against brother, and that before unbelievers (I Corinthians 6:1-6). (emphasis added)

Paul basically says that the *Church is supposed to judge the world*. The Church is the final *institutional* judge—not the State, but the Church. More important, Paul rebukes the Corinthians because they are not disciplining their own members. They aren't settling their own problems. So, trouble in the church is spilling out into society and allowing the State to intervene. The bottom line is that the State gets control and judges the Church, tantamount to judging *Christ*!

Church discipline is a powerful weapon against the State. It says to the government, "We're a separate kingdom, leave us alone."

How does church discipline work? Listen to the words of Christ.

> Moreover if your brother sins against you, go and tell him his fault between you and him alone. If he hears you, you have gained your brother. But if he will not hear you, take with you one or two more, that by the mouth of two or three witnesses every word may be established. And if he refuses to hear them, tell it to the church. But if he refuses even to hear the church, let him be to you like heathen and a tax collector. Assuredly, I say to you, whatever you bind on earth will be bound in heaven, and whatever you loose on earth will be loosed in heaven. Again I say to you that if two of you agree on earth concerning anything that they ask, it will be done for them by My Father in heaven. For where two or three are gathered together in My name, I am there in the midst of them (Matthew 18:15-20).

Here's the principle of "binding" we talked about at the beginning of the chapter. The Church can "bind" someone over and out of the congregation. Is this "unloving"? No, the Bible says that discipline is a supreme act of love. The writer to the Hebrews states, "And you have not forgotten the exhortation which speaks to you as to sons: My son, do not despise the chastening of the Lord, nor be discouraged when you are rebuked by Him; *for whom the Lord loves He chastens*, and scourges every son whom He receives" (Hebrews 12:5-6). (emphasis added)

If this is true of God, how much more should it be of the Church? Love is not contrary to discipline. Both go together. But the passage in Matthew lays out specific guidelines: (1) go privately; (2) then go with witnesses; (3) then take it to the whole church. How is this done? When the third stage of discipline is reached, the officers of the church should be brought in. They represent the church, and are the ones to handle the "tell it to the church." It may be that they will have to set up court and function like judges, just as Paul said in the 1 Corinthians 6 passage. If a guilty decision is reached and the person is still "unrepentant," then for his good and the well-being of the church, he must be put out.

But notice very carefully that the passage above says that the one who is cast out of the church is to "be to you *like* a heathen and a tax collector" (Matthew 18:17). Why doesn't the passage say the individual "is" a heathen? The Church rules "judicially," not "infallibly," meaning the excommunication hands over the guilty person to Satan. But the person might still be a believer. By being "declared" excommunicate, however, he is forced to face his eternal consequences if he does not repent. He is judicially dead and in the process of being brought back to life. Also, excommunication is only binding if the Church acts according to Scripture. If the Church is wrong, then the excommunication will not take. In either case, discipline is a "*legal* declaration."

Discipline is for the good of the church and society. Remember, Paul says that the failure to have "church courts" invites the State to put its court over the Church. The reverse is also true. When the Church handles its own discipline, it shows the State its boundaries. That's probably why the State wants to interfere with "Church discipline."

A couple of years ago, a church in Oklahoma excommunicated an unrepentant woman who was living in open adultery with a town official. She turned around and *sued the church*. The church lost in court. Why? The State doesn't want a disciplining Church, because a disciplining Church becomes influential in society. It becomes powerful enough to tell the State to stay out of the family and Church matters that are none of its business. Church discipline is just this powerful.

But, what if the State continues to try to stop church discipline? Is there nothing churches can do? No, there is another phase of discipline that can be put into effect.

Imprecatory Psalms

The Church (as an institution) is not allowed to use "carnal" weapons against the State. But this doesn't mean the Church is defenseless. God gives His people the most powerful weapon on earth, more powerful than atomic, or any other kind of "carnal" power. He gives His Church the *imprecatory psalms*.

An imprecatory psalm is a type of psalm that is a prayer of "malediction" ("speaking evil against") to be called down on the "enemies of the Church." Psalm 83 is a good example. Here is another:

> O Lord God, to whom vengeance belongs — O God to whom vengeance belongs, shine forth! Rise up, O Judge of the earth; render punishment to the proud. Lord, how long will the wicked, how long will the wicked triumph? . . . Who will rise up for me against the evildoers? Who will stand up for me against the workers of iniquity? Unless the Lord had been my help, My soul would soon have settled in silence. If I say, "My foot slips," Your mercy, O Lord, will hold me up. In the multitude of my anxieties within me, Your comforts delight my soul. Shall the throne of iniquity, which devises evil by law, have fellowship with You? They gather together against the life of the righteous, and condemn innocent blood. But the Lord has been my defense, and my God the rock of my refuge. He has brought on them their own iniquity. And shall cut them off in their own wickedness; The Lord God shall cut them off (Psalm 94:1-23).

The author begins this psalm with the very simple request that God would "punish" the wicked, the enemies of the kingdom of God. Is it right for a Christian to pray this way? Did not the Lord tell Christians to "pray for those who persecute you" (Matthew 5:44)?

First, Paul tells Christians to pray the *Psalms*, all of them. He says, "Speak to one another in *psalms* and hymns and other spiritual songs" (Ephesians 5:19). So, the *New Testament* definitely wants God's people to pray the *imprecatory psalms*. But what about Jesus' comment?

Second, Jesus tells us to "pray for our enemies," but He is specifically referring in that context to "personal" enemies, not necessarily enemies of the Church. Besides, the Psalms give us the *actual prayers* to be prayed, even if He is talking about "enemies of the Church." The *imprecatory psalms* are what the Church should pray. But keep in mind that discipline is *judicial*. In other words, the destruction of the wicked comes one of two ways: Actual destruction and *conversion*. That's right. God could destroy the wickedness of the State by converting it. He certainly did this to the Roman Empire under Constantine.

So, I encourage you to try to get your church to pray the imprecatory psalms, even in the *regular worship service as a congregation*. The psalms, remember, are supposed to be prayed by the Church. We're not to use these against our "personal" enemies. These are enemies of the *Church*!

Church discipline in the "maledictory" and inner-church forms is powerful. If the Church would use these, our world would change. Our society would leave the family alone and let the Church be its guardian.

Murray Norris of the Valley Christian University in Clovis, California illustrates the power of imprecatory psalms. He has been opposing pornography for years. Although he's an educator, he's an expert at fighting immorality. Cities and church groups regularly call him in to lead their local campaigns against pornography.

His success rate is phenomenal. He claims that if his eight steps are followed, pornography can be stopped in any situation. What's his secret? I don't know what he would say, but I think his success rate is due to one of those eight points that advocates the use of imprecatory psalms.

Usually the war against pornography boils down to a handful of decadent individuals who stand in the way of morality. Murray argues that above all else, pray that God would remove whoever stands in the way. Pray that they would either convert or be directly removed by God.

The results are powerful. Almost without exception, when an imprecatory prayer has been prayed, the antagonists against decency have retired, gotten sick (sometimes terminally ill), been beaten at the next election, or died!

Like God's covenantal signs of baptism and communion, however, the imprecatory psalms cut both ways: at those prayed against, and at the spiritual weakness of those who pray them. They are like hand grenades. If you don't intend to throw them, don't pull the pins.

Summary

I have presented what the Church can do to change society. Three points were made.

1. I called for true prophetic preaching, the kind that challenges society. It's the kind of preaching that proclaims and calls down the judgment of God.

2. I pointed out that faithful "weekly communion" would keep the Church from being condemned by the world. And, if the world gets off the Church's back, freedom comes to the family, especially the families in the Church.

3. I said that Church discipline distances the State from the Church. It's only when the Church fails to discipline its own members that the State can gain access. God says the Church will "judge the world," that is, if it disciplines its members.

Also, I explained a weapon of discipline, the *imprecatory psalms*, that the Church can use against the State. James says, "You do not have because you do not ask" (James 4:2). Isn't it time we ask God to put down the enemies of the Church by destruction or conversion?

The time *has* come. If the Church doesn't respond with at least these three plans of action, then our society will lose. We will lose. Our children will lose. And, the Church certainly will lose because "judgment begins at the house of the Lord" (1 Peter 4:17)!!!

13

WHAT CAN THE STATE DO?

Can the State do anything to put trusteeship of the family back into the parents' hands? Maybe you feel that it's a "lost cause." Maybe you think the State "can't legislate morality."

Fact: the State can't legislate anything *except* morality. All law is legislated morality. The law says "no" to some people who practice certain prohibited acts. These acts are prohibited because the legislators say they are immoral.

So the State *can* do something. Remember the early 1960s, when the "civil rights" issue broke loose? Did the government do something to change laws that prohibited blacks from eating and living around whites? You bet. *The government legislated morality.* The social, political, and most of all the attitudinal change came to a society that probably really didn't want the changes. But people complied, and people changed. In retrospect, they changed incredibly fast. Within a decade, the "Old South" was dead. The civil rights legislation accomplished something the Civil War's bloodshed didn't touch.

The timing was right: enough support to get the laws passed, enough guilt to weaken the resistance, and enough determination to push on through. A change in the law helped to change people's minds, but their attitudes had already been slowly undermined by a generation of ideological spade work.

This, in short, is what the Biblical Blueprints series is all about: ideological spade work. It will set the Christian agenda for the next generation, at least, and maybe this one.

The agenda I want to propose, however, moves in the direc-

156

tion of the *general public*, and against governmental officials.

How do I know? Take a look at the chart below. Appearing in *Family Building* (Regal Press, 1986), it compares a number of studies that polled *government and law and justice leaders*.

CONTRASTING THE GENERAL PUBLIC AND EVANGELICALS WITH THE GOVERNMENT AND LAW AND JUSTICE LEADERS (i.e. GALAJL)

*In *Gallup Survey* used weekly or greater.	GALLUP POLL GEN'L PUBLIC	GALLUP POLL-EVANG'S	CONN. MUTUAL GEN'L PUBLIC	CONN. MUTUAL GALAJL
Frequently* read the Bible	21%	84%	28%	10%
Never read the Bible	24%	0%	25%	46%
Frequently* encourages others to turn to religion	21%	47%	23%	6%
Has made a personal commitment to Christ	79%	93%	74%	22%
Frequently* attends church	36%	75%	44%	30%
Never attends church	22%	0%	18%	24%

Do you see what I see?

This chart indicates that our "representatives" are not representing even the "general public." In every category, the civil government is *way out of step*.

The average person, when it comes to religion, is much more concerned about "religious matters" than our politicians. The average person reads his Bible more. Almost half the representatives have *never read the Bible*. The average person encourages others to turn to religion more. A greater percentage of people have made a personal commitment than our politicians' responses indicate. A larger percentage of the general public attend church. Statistics say most government officials *never* attend church.

They stay home and watch television commentators instead, who also never go to church.

Is it any wonder our government is in such miserable shape?

When we come to the response of "evangelicals," as compared to the politicians, the contrast is unbelievably sharp.

So what? *Votes*, that's so what! There are an estimated 60 million evangelicals in this country. That's a huge number of people that could completely alter the political consensus as we know it. Believe me, the liberals know it.

I think it's time we start throwing our political weight around. But we've got to know what to say to the State. We need to make sure that we lay out a *Biblical agenda*. We have to work within the political arena with this agenda.

Nothing else will work when it comes to the State. If Christians want the State to change, they'll have to become *political stewards*. I don't mean they have to stop being spiritual. Heaven forbid. No, they will have to apply their spirituality to the political arena. For you to become a political steward, working within the political arena, you will have to take the following minimum steps.

1. Register to vote. You would be surprised how many Christians are not even registered to vote. The liberals go around in cars and round up people to register. You need to round up everyone in your Church and make sure he is registered. Tell your pastor to announce it from the pulpit. Have seminars on voting procedures. Learn when the voter registration deadlines fall.

2. Pick a party to work in. Try to choose a party that best represents your Christian beliefs. As of the moment, the Republican Party is the best choice because it is willing to incorporate *pro-life* resolutions in its party platform. If you happen to choose another party, make sure you think through a strategy for working your way to the top of the influential ladder. By the way, if you decide to become a "mole" inside a liberal party, realize that it will probably take much longer and a lot more patience. I don't recommend this approach unless you're extremely experienced and knowledgeable.

The long-term goal is to make every political party a self-consciously Christian party, just as it's the goal to make every institution self-consciously Christian. The goal is to subdue the whole earth. No loopholes, no escape hatches, no "king's x" from the King of kings. But it's easier to subdue your back yard before you subdue the Sahara desert. Practice in your back yard.

3. Attend precinct meetings. Our political system is designed to operate from the *bottom up*. Call the local party headquarters to find out what precinct you're in. You can probably find the party's

number in the telephone book. If not, then call the local Chamber of Commerce. When you call the party headquarters you want to work in, ask for a map of the precincts for the entire area. Take it to your church and ask the officers if you can post it on the bulletin board. This is just one more thing you can do to get Christians involved in politics.

Remember, all party resolutions begin at the precinct level. The party platform is set here. When you go to a precinct meeting you'll be impressed with how much power you, John-Q-Citizen, has in this country.

4. Get involved *working* for the party you've registered with. Recently, my wife and I learned an important lesson at our party's county convention. The chairman of the resolutions committee said to several Christians who were trying to get a strong pro-life resolution through, "I'm all for pro-life but the party wants to know if you people are just going to be 'one-issue' people, or if you're going to work for the party. Because if you're just 'single-issue' folks, you're not going to get the attention of the leadership." Whether you like this attitude or not, that's the way it is in any organization. Jesus gave us this principle: *dominion through service*. The people who roll up their shirtsleeves and work get listened to.

Hardly anyone is willing to work this way. Apathy rules the public, so the political professionals rule the public. That's why the American party system is a sitting duck.

Act like a steward of political power. You already are one, since you have the vote. There is no escape from this responsibility. It's like responding to the offer of the Gospel: *no decision is still a decision*. "I won't get involved!" is a decision—a decision to remain a political slave.

This is how the system works and can be changed. If you want to change it, you've got to do these four things. But now, let's get more specific.

Suggested Resolutions

If you want to change society at the civil level, you've got to use the existing political machinery. You've got to vote. But you've got to do more. This means getting *resolutions passed that can be made into laws.* At the local level, you can use your own precinct involvement to submit key resolutions. I've already suggested that the application of the capital offense laws would go a long way. But we're a "long way" from that happening. So, what should we push for in the mean time? In the following, I am suggesting 10 resolutions that are already being applied at the local precinct level in Texas, and winning.

Why the local and not the federal level? The present direction of our politics is shifting back to "State control." This is good, and it means that the way to affect your local situation best is through local expressions of political parties. *Forget about the federal level for the time being.* You can't win there anyway. But you *can* win at the local level. So, here are 10 suggested resolutions that will move our society closer to one that puts family trusteeship back into the hands of parents.

Resolution On Opposition To Minority Status For Homosexuals

WHEREAS, the practice of homosexuality is an abomination before God and is indicative of a society's moral decadence, and leads to the spread of severe diseases, such as AIDS; and

WHEREAS, the legalization of the practice of homosexuality would confer public acceptability to this activity and would lead inexorably to the breakdown of the traditional family unit and subsequently to the destruction of our nation; and

WHEREAS, state officials are refusing to defend anti-sodomy laws which are being challenged by the practitioners of homosexual conduct in the federal courts; now, therefore

BE IT RESOLVED, that the party in precinct #_____ calls upon the Governor and other state officials to defend the present anti-sodomy statutes against the challenge which it is experiencing in the federal courts, and further calls upon civil magistrates at all levels to denounce this activity and to maintain and strictly enforce laws prohibiting homosexual conduct; and

BE IT FURTHER RESOLVED, that homosexuality should not be taught or modeled as an alternate lifestyle in our public schools, nor should marriages between homosexuals, nor should the adoption of children by homosexuals be allowed in our State or Nation; and

BE IT FURTHER RESOLVED, that no person shall receive special legal entitlements or privileges based upon his sexual perversion.

We start where we are, in the society where we are. When the long-awaited revival comes, and millions are pulled into the Kingdom by God's Spirit, and when these new converts learn what God requires of the civil magistrates with respect to sodomy (God doesn't change His mind, after all), then we can deal even more severely with this sin. Today, we can't get any punitive measures. But we can keep sexual perversion away from the public sector through existing laws. We can get the existing laws enforced. That's a good first step.

AIDS has begun to change the public's view of homosexuality. Actually, the vast majority of Americans are revolted by homosexuality, and if they knew what *really* goes on between homosexuals, especially males, they would be more than revolted. Very few voters do know, because such unspeakable perversions cannot be mentioned in the commonly available press, and certainly not on television. The very level of perversion of the perverts at present shields them. Yet even what little the voters know appalls them.

They have been pushed into a confused, embarrassed, and *temporary* silence by all the loose talk about supposed Constitutional rights of sodomists — rights that every Constitutional lawyer knew didn't exist twenty years ago, let alone in the days of the Founding Fathers. But AIDS is getting public outrage out of the closet. AIDS is presently a politically protected disease, but it won't be for much longer. Voters are becoming much more willing to act — even if their motives are purely pragmatic.

It now costs an average of $140,000 in tax dollars to care for each AIDS victim in a public hospital, and it's money down the drain. Every single one of them dies within two years. There is no cure. All our public hospitals will be filled with nothing but AIDS victims if the rate of increase in AIDS victims continues for ten more years. This will literally bankrupt the public health budgets of the major cities within just a few years. It will create the setting for a moral and political revolution, an effect that bankrupt public treasuries usually create. Christians will then use this marvelous opportunity to move society closer to a Biblical solution—a solution that protects the family. Meanwhile, we position ourselves as the one group that sounded the alarm in advance.

Some Christians may say that this is an unloving, uncharitable attitude. *These Christians are embarrassed by God*, and embarrassed by the specific requirements that God has clearly set forth with respect to society's legitimate and proper control of homosexual behavior (Leviticus 20:13). This embarrassment about God's laws will be gone before this century ends. When AIDS begins to hit the American heterosexual community, as it now has in Africa, and when the terror comes close to Christian homes, and when there is no room in hospitals for sick Christians, then today's hesitant, soft-hearted Christians will change their minds and stop apologizing for God's supposed harshness.

A worldwide social and religious transformation is coming, in the form of a virus. Christians and non-Christian heterosexuals are about to learn what the penalty is for being embarrassed by God's civil law and refusing to impose it. The penalty is visible judgment. There is nothing like God's visible judgment to firm up practical Christian theology. There is also nothing like it for weakening (or even eliminating) God's opponents.

This may sound radical today. In 1995, it will sound too soft.

Resolution On Taxes

BE IT RESOLVED, that the party in Precinct #_____ opposes a state income tax and any new kinds of taxes or additional tax increases on the State or local levels.

I have spent an entire chapter of this book discussing how a graduated tax system has hurt the family. If your state has an income tax, you've got to get rid of it. If nothing else, *freeze* taxation. Many reliable sources say that if we can just *freeze* taxation, we'll be able to win eventually. Remember, as long as the State has a graduated tax structure, you're going to have a difficult time accumulating a decent inheritance for your family.

Resolution On The Sovereignty Of The Family

BE IT RESOLVED, that the party in Precinct #_____ recognizes that the monogamous family is a God-ordained institution and is one of the foundational units of society. The family is primarily responsible for the welfare, education, and property of its members. (The family is defined as those related by blood, marriage or adoption.) All attempts to weaken or destroy the family, including no-fault divorce, desertion, pornography, homosexuality, adultery, and numerous forms of governmental interference and control over the family must be opposed.

This resolution is a definition of the family that protects its Biblical prerogatives. If you can get this one through, you'll neutralize a lot of legislation against the family.

Resolution On Pro-Life

WHEREAS, God is the author of life and that human life originates at conception; now therefore,
BE IT RESOLVED, by the party in Precinct #_____ that abortion must be opposed as the shedding of innocent blood which will surely bring God's judgement upon our nation; that a Human Life Amendment to the U.S. Constitution must be adopted by the U.S. Congress to protect innocent human life from the point of conception until the time of natural death; and that we call upon our State Legislature to pass appropriate legislation to this end.

Let's face it, even if the Congress passes a pro-life law, it will have to be adopted by the individual states. The battle is going to boil down to your local community. Regardless of what the Feds do, the local citizenry will have to re-criminalize abortion.

Resolution On Non-State Schools

WHEREAS, education is the primary responsibility of parents, and that parents, not the state, are the stewards of the children, now therefore,
BE IT RESOLVED, that the party in Precinct #_____ opposes all attempts by the state or local government to interfere with parental rights in education; and that we further support main-

taining the present status of private, parochial, and home schools free from state government control.

You should know by now that the entrenched, tax-supported, humanist State bureaucrats want to control what your children learn. It's probably the biggest fight today between the family and the State. You've got to push for positive legislation that will protect your right—even if you don't want to use it—to educate your own children without governmental control. If you don't, then the government will control everything. It's an all or nothing battle!

Resolution On Right-To-Work

WHEREAS, any individual should have the freedom to bid competitively for any job he desires without being forced to join or pay dues to any organization as a condition of employment; therefore

BE IT RESOLVED, by the party in Precinct #_____ that the State of _____ institute, or maintain a Right-To-Work Law.

What happens to a family if its members, particularly the parents, are not able to work without oppression? They're severely inhibited. Unfortunately, the government seems to be in the business of all kinds of oppression. That's why it protects labor unions in many states. We don't advocate government anti-union activity. We just advocate a man's legal immunity from persecution or violence if he bids on a job. If you want freedom for the family, you've got to push for the right-to-work, by which we mean "right to *bid*."

Resolution On Opposing Gun Control

BE IT RESOLVED, that the party of Precinct #_____ reaffirms the right of American citizens to keep and bear arms, as guaranteed by the second amendment of the U.S. Constitution, and opposes any and all legislation which would restrict that right.

You can't expect to preserve the traditional family if you can't protect it. Keep in mind that Communism is rapidly coming close to American borders in Mexico. Keep in mind that we live in a violent society. Keep in mind that there are not enough policemen to respond quickly enough if thugs attack your house. One man said in our last precinct meeting, "If I have a gun, I feel that I can do at least *something* to protect my family if it's attacked. But one thing is for certain if I don't have a gun—I can't do much of anything." Another man said, "I have never owned a gun and don't plan to. But I think I have the right to own one in the event that I want to."

When guns are outlawed, only outlaws will own guns. The Constitution says that law-abiding citizens shouldn't have to become outlaws with respect to gun ownership.

Resolution On Victim's Rights

WHEREAS, the federal and state judiciary have exhibited an inordinate concern for the right of criminals, as opposed to the rights of those who have been the victims of criminals and their crimes; and

WHEREAS, this has led to a disrespect for law which threatens to undermine the very foundations of our society; now therefore

BE IT RESOLVED by the party in Precinct #_____ that restitution should be instituted so that victims of crime are compensated by those who perpetrate crimes against them, for injuries and losses to their person and private property; and that capital punishment be meted out to those whose crimes are capital in nature.

Jails aren't Biblical. Restitution is Biblical. Jails are training centers for crime, and they will soon become distribution centers for AIDS.

Fines to the State aren't Biblical, except to be used to compensate victims of unsolved criminal acts. Criminals should pay money to their victims, not to the State. Crime is personal; compensation should be personal. The State is to promote justice, not to become a self-financing bureaucracy.

As I've already said, you're not going to be able to get the

Biblical death penalties re-instituted "overnight." But this approach is designed to change the emphasis of law from reform to restitution. The Biblical position is that people are best reformed by having to pay restitution, instead of being incarcerated.

Resolution On The Sovereignty Of The Church

BE IT RESOLVED, that the party in Precinct #_____ acknowledges that the Church is a God-ordained institution with a sphere of authority separate from that of civil government and thus the Church is not to be regulated, controlled or taxed by any level of civil government.

Remember, historically the Church has been the best "buffer-zone" between the family and the State. Nothing can protect the family better. So, what happens to the Church indirectly affects the family. This is why the State is simultaneously attacking the family and the Church.

The resolution above is designed to remove *all* regulations off the Church. Again, on this issue it's an *all or nothing proposition*. If the State is allowed to regulate the Church at all, then it has the power to regulate everything!

Resolution On The Legitimate Function Of Civil Government

WHEREAS, God is Sovereign over all the world and has divinely instituted civil government among men, for His own glory and for the public good, and for the administration of this institution He has ordained civil rulers to exercise their authority under Him in obedience to His laws in order to promote justice, restrain wickedness, punish evildoers, and protect the life, liberty, and private property of the citizens, and provide for domestic and national defense; and

WHEREAS, when civil government assumes responsibilities and authority beyond this well delineated scope it occurs at the expense of the other God-ordained institutions, the Family and the Church; now therefore,

BE IT RESOLVED, that the party in Precinct #_____ supports this historic concept, established by our nation's Founding Fathers, of limited civil government jurisdiction under the laws of

God and repudiates the humanistic doctrine that the state is sovereign over the affairs of men and over the Family and the Church.

It is necessary to re-educate the populace on the proper Biblical and Constitutional role of the State. Our problem is that most people are ignorant. This resolution will do a lot of educating. It intends, however, to *limit* government and make a strong statement against the present humanistic view of the State: the one that has stripped Family and Church of their Biblical responsibilities.

Here are 10 resolutions that you can take to your precinct meetings. Study them. Propose them when the opportunity arises. They don't have to be introduced at the first precinct meeting. They may not all be politically acceptable in your state. Get what you can. Don't appear to be a red-hot, especially an amateur red-hot. Gain their confidence. We are slicing salami, one piece at a time, just like our opponents did. God will drive out our enemies slowly, year by year, just as He promised the Israelites (Exodus 23:27-30). Bide your time.

Probably, by the time you read this book you will have several months before the next precinct meeting in your area. That's not a problem because you may have to take a crash course in civics to understand how local government works. Also, don't worry if you have to modify these resolutions for your local situation. For your information, they were originally drafted by the Texas Grassroots Coalition, Inc. It is a Christian political action group that lobbies and gets information out to Christians and other concerned citizens. If you want to start a similar version or find out how to modify their resolutions to fit your state situation, write them. Send a check to cover their expenses. There are no free lunches in political reform movements. Here is their address.

Texas Grassroots Coalition, Inc.
9501 Capital of Texas North
Suite 304
Austin, Texas 78759

There also is a specialized program that trains people in details of getting elected to public office. I have decided not to go public with the name and address of this organization. It is listed in the Biblical Blueprints book on politics: *Liberator of the Nations*, by Dennis Peacocke. Don't grab for the robes of authority prematurely, as Adam did. Your first goal is to get involved in local precinct politics, not run for Congress. First things first.

Summary

I've told you how to become a political steward to change the State. If you want to change civil laws that will put trusteeship of the family back in the family's hands, you're going to have to get involved in politics. The State is a political organism and there's no way to change it from the outside. Sure you can write letters, but that's not going to change things. So, I told you about four simple steps to get involved:

1. Register to vote.
2. Pick a party to work with.
3. Get involved in your local precinct.
4. Work for your local party and gain influence.

To be even more specific, I gave you 10 resolutions to push for at your local precinct meetings. They're not the last word, but a place to begin to implement a Biblical view of the family in society. They were originally framed by the Texas Grassroots Coalition, Inc.

I think everyone can do these things. If you're not willing to take these steps, however, you'll only have yourself to blame if the State takes complete control of your children, family, and future. If you've learned anything from this book, I hope you understand that you can't protect the family by familism. You can't save your family by locking yourself up with your own family and hiding from the world. You've got to act on several fronts. There's a war on the family. It's under siege. If you act, you can help bring the family back to a place of real influence. But, you've got to take what you've learned in this book and *act now!!*

Oh, yes: I nearly forgot. Never, ever vote "yes" on a school bond proposal. No more long-term debt, which is against the Bible (Deuteronomy 15; Romans 13:8). If 60 million American Christians automatically voted "no" on every school bond proposal, we would get the immediate attention of the education bureaucrats. We would directly affect their wallets.

Finally, if you run for the public school board, do it with one intention only: to create an orderly transition to exclusively private education. If you can't be elected on this platform (as seems likely), then become the candidate who wants to reduce waste. (The Biblical definition of wasteful public schools: "public schools.") Your real agenda: no more pay increases for teachers, no more school building programs, and a reduction next year in property taxes. Forever.

Until the last public school superintendant is strangled in the non-negotiable demands of the last National Education Association union president, the humanists' war against the family isn't over!!!

BIBLIOGRAPHY

Adams, J. E. *Christian Living in the Home*. Phillipsburg, New Jersey: Presbyterian and Reformed, 1972.

Adams, Blair, and Stein, Joel. *Who Owns the Child*. Grand Junction, Colorado: Truth Forum, 1983.

Bromiley, Geoffrey. *God and Marriage*. Grand Rapids: Eerdmans, 1980.

Johnston, O. R. *Who Needs the Family?*. Downers Grove, Ilinois: InterVarsity Press, 1979.

Kilpatrick, William Kirk. *Psychological Seduction*. Nashville: Thomas Nelson, 1983.

Morgan, Edmund, S. *The Puritan Family*. New York: Harper & Row, 1944.

Murray, Charles. *Losing Ground: American Social Policy 1950-1980*. New York: Basic Books, 1984.

Plymouth Rock Foundation. *Biblical Principles*. Plymouth, Massachussetts: Plymouth Rock Foundation, 1984.

Robison, James. *Attack on the Family*. Wheaton, Illinois: Tyndale House, 1980.

Whitehead, John, W. *Parents' Rights*. Westchester, Illinois: Crossway Books, 1985.

SCRIPTURE INDEX

OLD TESTAMENT

NEW TESTAMENT

SUBJECT INDEX

WHAT ARE BIBLICAL BLUEPRINTS?
by Gary North

How many times have you heard this one?

"The Bible isn't a textbook of . . ."

You've heard it about as many times as you' ve heard this one:

"The Bible doesn't provide blueprints for . . ."

The odd fact is that some of the people who assure you of this are Christians. Nevertheless, if you ask them, "Does the Bible have answers for the problems of life?" you'll get an unqualified "yes" for an answer.

Question: If the Bible isn't a textbook, and if it doesn't provide blueprints, then just how, specifically and concretely, does it provide answers for life's problems? Either it answers real-life problems, or it doesn't.

In short: *Does the Bible make a difference*?

Let's put it another way. If a mass revival at last hits this nation, and if millions of people are regenerated by God's grace through faith in the saving work of Jesus Christ at Calvary, will this change be visible in the way the new converts run their lives? Will their politics change, their business dealings change, their families change, their family budgets change, and their church membership change?

In short: Will conversion make a visible difference in our personal lives? If not, why not?

Second, two or three years later, will Congress be voting for a different kind of defense policy, foreign relations policy, environmental policy, immigration policy, monetary policy, and so forth?

181

Will the Federal budget change? If not, why not?

In short: Will conversion to Christ make a visible difference in our civilization? If not, why not?

The Great Commission

What the Biblical Blueprints Series is attempting to do is to outline what some of that visible difference in our culture ought to be. The authors are attempting to set forth, in clear language, *fundamental Biblical principles* in numerous specific areas of life. The authors are not content to speak in vague generalities. These books not only set forth explicit principles that are found in the Bible and derived from the Bible, they also offer specific practical suggestions about what things need to be changed, and how Christians can begin programs that will produce these many changes.

The authors see the task of American Christians just as the Puritans who came to North America in the 1630's saw their task: *to establish a city on a hill* (Matthew 5:14). The authors want to see a Biblical reconstruction of the United States, so that it can serve as an example to be followed all over the world. They believe that God's principles are tools of evangelism, to bring the nations to Christ. The Bible promises us that these principles will produce such good fruit that the whole world will marvel (Deuteronomy 4:5-8). When nations begin to marvel, they will begin to soften to the message of the gospel. What the authors are calling for is *comprehensive revival*—a revival that will transform everything on earth.

In other words, the authors are calling Christians to obey God and take up the Great Commission: to *disciple* (discipline) all the nations of the earth (Matthew 28:19).

What each author argues is that there are God-required principles of thought and practice in areas that some people today believe to be outside the area of "religion." What Christians should know by now is that *nothing* lies outside religion. God is judging all of our thoughts and acts, judging our institutions, and working through human history to bring this world to a final judgment.

We present the case that God offers *comprehensive salvation* — regeneration, healing, restoration, and the obligation of total social reconstruction — because the world is in *comprehensive sin*.

To judge the world it is obvious that God has to have standards. If there were no absolute standards, there could be no earthly judgment, and no final judgment because men could not be held accountable.

(Warning: these next few paragraphs are very important. They are the base of the entire Blueprints series. It is important that you understand my reasoning. I really believe that if you understand it, you will agree with it.)

To argue that God's standards don't apply to everything is to argue that sin hasn't affected and infected everything. To argue that God's Word doesn't give us a revelation of God's requirements for us is to argue that we are flying blind as Christians. It is to argue that there are *zones of moral neutrality* that God will not judge, either today or at the day of judgment, because these zones somehow are *outside His jurisdiction*. In short, "no law-no jurisdiction."

But if God *does* have jurisdiction over the whole universe, which is what every Christian believes, then there must be universal standards by which God executes judgment. The authors of this series argue for God's *comprehensive judgment*, and we declare His *comprehensive salvation*. We therefore are presenting a few of His *comprehensive blueprints*.

The Concept of Blueprints

An architectural blueprint gives us the structural requirements of a building. A blueprint isn't intended to tell the owner where to put the furniture or what color to paint the rooms. A blueprint does place limits on where the furniture and appliances should be put — laundry here, kitchen there, etc. — but it doesn't take away our personal options based on personal taste. A blueprint just specifies what must be done during construction for the building to do its job and to survive the test of time. It gives direction to the contractor. Nobody wants to be on the twelfth floor of a building that collapses.

Today, we are unquestionably on the twelfth floor, and maybe even the fiftieth. Most of today's "buildings" (institutions) were designed by humanists, for use by humanists, but paid for mostly by Christians (investments, donations, and taxes). These "buildings" aren't safe. Christians (and a lot of non-Christians) now are hearing the creaking and groaning of these tottering buildings. Millions of people have now concluded that it's time to: (1) call in a totally new team of foundation and structural specialists to begin a complete renovation, or (2) hire the original contractors to make at least temporary structural modifications until we can all move to safer quarters, or (3) call for an emergency helicopter team because time has just about run out, and the elevators aren't safe either.

The writers of this series believe that the first option is the wise one: Christians need to rebuild the foundations, using the Bible as their guide. This view is ignored by those who still hope and pray for the third approach: God's helicopter escape. Finally, those who have faith in minor structural repairs don't tell us what or where these hoped-for safe quarters are, or how humanist contractors are going to build them any safer next time.

Why is it that some Christians say that God hasn't drawn up any blueprints? If God doesn't give us blueprints, then who does? If God doesn't set the permanent standards, then who does? If God hasn't any standards to judge men by, then who judges man?

The humanists' answer is inescapable: *man* does — autonomous, design-it-yourself, do-it-yourself man. Christians call this man-glorifying religion the religion of humanism. It is amazing how many Christians until quite recently have believed humanism's first doctrinal point, namely, that God has not established permanent blueprints for man and man's institutions. Christians who hold such a view of God's law serve as *humanism's chaplains*.

Men are God's appointed "contractors." We were never supposed to draw up the blueprints, but we *are* supposed to execute them, in history and then after the resurrection. Men have been given dominion on the earth to subdue it for God's glory. "So God created man in His own image; in the image of God He created him; male and female He created them. Then God blessed them, and God said to them, 'Be fruitful and multiply; fill the earth and subdue it; have dominion over the fish of the sea, over the birds of the air, and over every living thing that moves on the earth'" (Genesis 1:27-28).

Christians about a century ago decided that God never gave them the responsibility to do any building (except for churches). That was just what the humanists had been waiting for. They immediately stepped in, took over the job of contractor ("Someone has to do it!"), and then announced that they would also be in charge of drawing up the blueprints. We can see the results of a similar assertion in Genesis, chapter 11: the tower of Babel. Do you remember God's response to that particular humanistic public works project?

Never Be Embarrassed By the Bible

This sounds simple enough. Why should Christians be embarrassed by the Bible? But they *are* embarrassed . . . millions of them. The humanists have probably done more to slow down the spread of the gospel by convincing Christians to be embarrassed by the Bible than by any other strategy they have adopted.

Test your own thinking. Answer this question: "Is God mostly a God of love or mostly a God of wrath?" Think about it before you answer.

It's a trick question. The Biblical answer is: "God is equally a God of love and a God of wrath." But Christians these days will generally answer almost automatically, "God is mostly a God of love, not wrath."

Now in their hearts, they know this answer can't be true. God sent His Son to the cross to die. His own Son! That's how much God hates sin. That's wrath with a capital "W."

But why did He do it? Because He loves His Son, and those who follow His Son. So, you just can't talk about the wrath of God without talking about the love of God, and vice versa. The cross is the best proof we have: God is both wrathful and loving. Without the fires of hell as the reason for the cross, the agony of Jesus Christ on the cross was a mistake, a case of drastic overkill.

What about heaven and hell? We know from John's vision of the day of judgment, "Death and Hades [hell] were cast into the lake of fire. This is the second death. And anyone not found written in the Book of Life was cast into the lake of fire" (Revelation 20:14-15).

Those whose names are in the Book of Life spend eternity with God in their perfect, sin-free, resurrected bodies. The Bible calls this the New Heaven and the New Earth.

Now, which is more eternal, the lake of fire, or the New Heaven and the New Earth? Obviously, they are both eternal. So, God's wrath is equally ultimate with His love throughout eternity. *Christians all admit this*, but sometimes only under extreme pressure. And that is precisely the problem.

For over a hundred years, theological liberals have blathered on and on about the love of God. But when you ask them, "What about hell?" they start dancing verbally. If you press them, they eventually deny the existence of eternal judgment. We *must* understand: they have no doctrine of the total love of God because they have no doctrine of the total wrath of God. They can't really understand what it is that God is His grace offers us in Christ because they refuse to admit what eternal judgment tells us about the character of God.

The doctrine of eternal fiery judgment is by far the most unacceptable doctrine in the Bible, as far as hell-bound humanists are concerned. They can't believe that Christians can believe in such a horror. But we do. We must. This belief is the foundation of Christian evangelism. It is the motivation for Christian foreign missions. We shouldn't be surprised that the God-haters would like us to drop this doctrine. When Christians believe it, they make too much trouble for God's enemies.

So if we believe in this doctrine, the doctrine above all others that ought to embarrass us before humanists, then why do we start to squirm when God-hating people ask us: "Well, what kind of God would require the death penalty? What kind of God would send a plague (or other physical judgment) on people, the way He sent one on the Israelites, killing 70,000 of them, even though they had done nothing wrong, just because David had conducted a military census in peacetime (2 Samuel 24:10-16)? What kind of God sends AIDS?" The proper answer: "The God of the Bible, *my* God."

Compared to the doctrine of eternal punishment, what is some two-bit judgment like a plague? Compared to eternal screaming agony in the lake of fire, without hope of escape, what is the death penalty? The liberals try to embarrass us about these earthly "down payments" on God's final judgment because they want to rid the world of the idea of final judgment. So they insult the character of God, and also the character of Christians, by sneering at the Bible's account of who God is, what He has done in history, and what He requires from men.

Are you tired of their sneering? I know I am.

Nothing in the Bible should be an embarrassment to any Christian. We may not know for certain precisely how some Biblical truth or historic event should be properly applied in our day, but every historic record, law, announcement, prophecy, judgment, and warning in the Bible is the very Word of God, and is not to be flinched at by anyone who calls himself by Christ's name.

We must never doubt that whatever God did in the Old Testament era, the Second Person of the Trinity also did. God's counsel and judgments are not divided. We must be careful not to regard Jesus Christ as a sort of "unindicted co-conspirator" when we read the Old Testament. "For whoever is ashamed of Me and My words in this adulterous and sinful generation, of him the Son of Man also will be ashamed when He comes in the glory of His Father with the holy angels" (Mark 8:38).

My point here is simple. If we as Christians can accept what is a very hard principle of the Bible, that Christ was a blood sacrifice for our individual sins, then we shouldn't flinch at accepting any of the rest of God's principles. As we joyfully accepted His salvation, so we must joyfully embrace all of His principles that affect any and every area of our lives.

The Whole Bible

When, in a court of law, the witness puts his hand on the Bible and swears to tell the truth, the whole truth, and nothing but the truth, so help him God, he thereby swears on the Word of God — the *whole* Word of God, and *nothing but* the Word of God. The Bible is a unit. It's a "package deal." The New Testament doesn't overturn the Old Testament; it's a *commentary* on the Old Testament. It tells us how to use the Old Testament properly in the period after the death and resurrection of Israel's messiah, God's Son.

Jesus said: "Do not think that I came to destroy the Law or the Prophets. I did not come to destroy but to fulfill. For assuredly, I say to you, till heaven and earth pass away, one jot or one tittle will by no means pass from the law till all is fulfilled. Whoever therefore breaks one of the least of these commandments, and teaches men to do so, shall be called least in the kingdom of heaven; but whoever does and teaches them, he shall be called great in the kingdom of heaven" (Matthew 5:17-19). The Old Testament isn't a discarded first draft of God's Word. It isn't "God's Word emeritus."

Dominion Christianity teaches that there are four covenants under God, meaning four kinds of *vows* under God: personal (individual), and the three institutional covenants: ecclesiastical (the church), civil (governments), and family. All other human institutions (business, educational, charitable, etc.) are to one degree or other under the jurisdiction of these four covenants. No single covenant is absolute; therefore, no single institution is all-powerful. Thus, Christian liberty is *liberty under God and God's law.*

Christianity therefore teaches pluralism, but a very special kind of pluralism: plural institutions under God's comprehensive law. It does not teach a pluralism of law structures, or a pluralism of moralities, for as we will see shortly, this sort of ultimate pluralism (as distinguished from *institutional* pluralism) is always either polytheistic or humanistic. Christian people are required to take dominion over the earth by means of all these God-ordained institutions, not just the church, or just the state, or just the family.

The kingdom of God includes every human institution, and every aspect of life, for all of life is under God and is governed by His unchanging principles. All of life is under God and God's principles because God intends to *judge* all of life *in terms of* His principles.

In this structure of *plural governments*, the institutional churches serve as *advisors* to the other institutions (the Levitical function), but the churches can only pressure individual leaders through the threat of excommunication. As a restraining factor on unwarranted church authority, an unlawful excommunication by one local church or denomination is always subject to review by the others if and when the excommunicated person seeks membership elsewhere. Thus, each of the three covenantal institutions is to be run under God, as interpreted by its lawfully elected or ordained leaders, with the advice of the churches, not the compulsion.

Majority Rule

Just for the record, the authors aren't in favor of imposing some sort of top-down bureaucratic tyranny in the name of Christ. The kingdom of God requires a bottom-up society. The bottom-up Christian society rests ultimately on the doctrine of *self*-government under God. It's the humanist view of society that promotes top-down bureaucratic power.

The authors are in favor evangelism and missions leading to a widespread Christian revival, so that the great mass of earth's inhabitants will place themselves under Christ's protection, and voluntarily use His covenantal principles for self-government. Christian reconstruction begins with personal conversion to Christ and self-government under God's principles, then spreads to others through revival, and only later brings comprehensive changes in civil law, when the vast majority of voters voluntarily agree to live under Biblical blueprints.

Let's get this straight: Christian reconstruction depends on majority rule. Of course, the leaders of the Christian reconstructionist movement expect a majority eventually to accept Christ as savior. If this doesn't happen, then Christians must be content with only partial reconstruction, and only partial blessings from

God. It isn't possible to ramrod God's blessings from the top down, unless you're God. Only humanists think that man is God. All we're trying to do is get the ramrod away from them, and melt it down. The melted ramrod could then be used to make a great grave marker for humanism: "The God That Failed."

The Continuing Heresy of Dualism

Many (of course, not all!) of the objections to the material in this book series will come from people who have a worldview that is very close to an ancient church problem: dualism. A lot of well-meaning Christian people are dualists, although they don't even know what it is.

Dualism teaches that the world is inherently divided: spirit vs. matter, or law vs. mercy, or mind vs. matter, or nature vs. grace. What the Bible teaches is that this world is divided *ethically* and *personally*: Satan vs. God, right vs. wrong. The conflict between God and Satan will end at the final judgment. Whenever Christians substitute some other form of dualism for ethical dualism, they fall into heresy and suffer the consequences. That's what has happened today. We are suffering from revived versions of ancient heresies.

Marcion's Dualism

The Old Testament was written by the same God who wrote the New Testament. There were not two Gods in history, meaning there was no dualism or radical split between the two testamental periods. There is only one God, in time and eternity.

This idea has had opposition throughout church history. An ancient two-Gods heresy was first promoted in the church about a century after Christ's crucifixion, and the church has always regarded it as just that, a heresy. It was proposed by a man named Marcion. Basically, this heresy teaches that there are two completely different law systems in the Bible: Old Testament law and New Testament law (or non-law). But Marcion took the logic of his position all the way. He argued that two law systems means two Gods. The God of wrath wrote the Old Testament, and the God of mercy wrote the New Testament. In short: "two laws-two Gods."

Many Christians still believe something dangerously close to Marcionism: not a two-Gods view, exactly, but a God-who-changed-all-His-rules sort of view. They begin with the accurate teaching that the ceremonial laws of the Old Testament were fulfilled by Christ, and therefore that the *unchanging principles* of Biblical worship are *applied differently* in the New Testament. But then they erroneously conclude that the whole Old Testament system of civil law was dropped by God, and *nothing Biblical was put in its place*. In other words, God created a sort of vacuum for state law.

This idea turns civil law-making over to Satan. In our day, this means that civil law-making is turned over to humanists. *Christians have unwittingly become the philosophical allies of the humanists with respect to civil law.* With respect to their doctrine of the state, therefore, most Christians hold what is in effect a two-Gods view of the Bible.

Gnosticism's Dualism

Another ancient heresy that is still with us is gnosticism. It became a major threat to the early church almost from the beginning. It was also a form of dualism, a theory of a radical split. The gnostics taught that the split is between evil matter and good spirit. Thus, their goal was to escape this material world through other-worldly exercises that punish the body. They believed in *retreat from the world of human conflicts and responsibility.* Some of these ideas got into the church, and people started doing ridiculous things. One "saint" sat on a platform on top of a pole for several decades. This was considered very spiritual. (Who fed him? Who cleaned up after him?)

Thus, many Christians came to view "the world" as something permanently outside the kingdom of God. They believed that this hostile, forever-evil world cannot be redeemed, reformed, and reconstructed. Jesus didn't really die for it, and it can't be healed. At best, it can be subdued by power (maybe). This dualistic view of the world vs. God's kingdom narrowly restricted any earthly manifestation of God's kingdom. Christians who were influenced by gnosticism concluded that God's kingdom refers only to the institutional church. They argued that the institutional church is the *only* manifestation of God's kingdom.

This led to two opposite and equally evil conclusions. *First*, power religionists ("salvation through political power") who accepted this definition of God's kingdom tried to put the institutional church in charge of everything, since it is supposedly "the only manifestation of God's kingdom on earth." To subdue the supposedly unredeemable world, which is forever outside the kingdom, the institutional church has to rule with the sword. A single, monolithic institutional church then gives orders to the state, and the state must without question enforce these orders with the sword. The hierarchy of the institutional church concentrates political and economic power. *What then becomes of liberty?*

Second, escape religionists ("salvation is exclusively internal") who also accepted this narrow definition of the kingdom sought refuge from the evil world of matter and politics by fleeing to hide inside the institutional church, an exclusively "spiritual kingdom," now narrowly defined. They abandoned the world to evil tyrants. *What then becomes of liberty?* What becomes of the idea of God's progressive restoration of all things under Jesus Christ? What, finally, becomes of the idea of Biblical dominion?

When Christians improperly narrow their definition of the kingdom of God, the visible influence of this comprehensive kingdom (both spiritual and institutional at the same time) begins to shrivel up. The first heresy leads to tyranny *by* the church, and the second heresy leads to tyranny *over* the church. Both of these narrow definitions of God's kingdom destroy the liberty of the responsible Christian man, self-governed under God and God's law.

Zoroaster's Dualism

The last ancient pagan idea that still lives on is also a variant of dualism: matter vs. spirit. It teaches that God and Satan, good and evil, are forever locked in combat, and that good never triumphs over evil. The Persian religion of Zoroastrianism has held such a view for over 2,500 years. The incredibly popular "Star Wars" movies were based on this view of the world: the "dark" side of "the force" against its "light" side. In modern versions of this ancient dualism, the "force" is usually seen as itself impersonal: individuals personalize either the dark side or the light side by "plugging into" its power.

There are millions of Christians who have adopted a very pessimistic version of this dualism, though not in an impersonal form. God's kingdom is battling Satan's, and God's is losing. History isn't going to get better. In fact, things are going to get a lot worse externally. Evil will visibly push good into the shadows. The church is like a band of soldiers who are surrounded by a huge army of Indians. "We can't win boys, so hold the fort until Jesus comes to rescue us!"

That doesn't sound like Abraham, Moses, Joshua, Gideon, and David, does it? Christians read to their children one of the children's favorite stories, David and Goliath, yet in their own lives, millions of Christian parents really think that the Goliaths of this world are the unbeatable earthly winners. Christians haven't even picked up a stone.

Until very recently.

An Agenda for Victory

The change has come since 1980. Many Christians' thinking has shifted. Dualism, gnosticism, and "God changed His program midstream" ideas have begun to be challenged. The politicians have already begun to reckon with the consequences. Politicians are the people we pay to raise their wet index fingers in the wind to sense a shift, and they have sensed it. It scares them, too. It should.

A new vision has captured the imaginations of a growing army of registered voters. This new vision is simple: it's the old vision of Genesis 1:27-28 and Matthew 28:19-20. It's called *dominion*.

Four distinct ideas must be present in any ideology that ex pects to overturn the existing view of the world and the existing social order:

    A doctrine of ultimate truth (permanence)
    A doctrine of providence (confidence)
    Optimism toward the future (motivation)
    Binding comprehensive law (reconstruction)

The Marxists have had such a vision, or at least those Marxists who don't live inside the bureaucratic giants called the Soviet Union and Red China. The radical (please, not "fundamentalist") Muslims of Iran also have such a view.

Now, for the first time in over 300 years, Bible-believing Christians have rediscovered these four points in the theology of Christianity. For the first time in over 300 years, a growing number of Christians are starting to view themselves as an army on the move. This army will grow. This series is designed to help it grow. And grow tougher.

The authors of this series are determined to set the agenda in world affairs for the next few centuries. We know where the permanent answers are found: in the Bible, and *only* in the Bible. We believe that we have begun to discover at least preliminary answers to the key questions. There may be better answers, clearer answers, and more orthodox answers, but they must be found in the Bible, not at Harvard University or on the CBS Evening News.

We are self-consciously firing the opening shot. We are calling the whole Christian community to join with us in a very serious debate, just as Luther called them to debate him when he nailed the 95 theses to the church door, over four and a half centuries ago.

It is through such an exchange of ideas by those who take the Bible seriously that a nation and a civilization can be saved. There are now 5 billion people in the world. If we are to win our world (and these billions of souls) for Christ we must lift up the message of Christ by becoming the city on the hill. When the world sees the blessings by God upon a nation run by His principles, the mass conversion of whole nations to the Kingdom of our Lord will be the most incredible in of all history.

If we're correct about the God-required nature of our agenda, it will attract a dedicated following. It will produce a social transformation that could dwarf the Reformation. This time, we're not limiting our call for reformation to the institutional church.

This time, we mean business.

Geneva Ministries
P.O. Box 131300
Tyler, TX 75713

Gentlemen:

I just finished reading Ray Sutton's *Who Owns the Family?* I understand that your organization makes available several newsletters that include articles by Rev. Sutton, as well as articles by James B. Jordan, George Grant, David Chilton, and Gary DeMar. Please send me additional information and put me on your mailing list.

_____
name

_____
address

_____
city, state, zip

_____
area code and phone number

☐ Enclosed is a tax-deductible donation to help meet expenses.

RAY SUTTON'S FAMILY NEWSLETTER

Legacy
P.O. Box 7337
Tyler, TX 75711

Dear Mr. Sutton:

I want more of what I've been reading in your book. Please send me one subscription (12 monthly issues) of your family newsletter. I desire more of your solid and practical material on the family. I need it not just for myself but for my whole family . . . for *their* future. I understand that this tear-out sheet entitles me to a $5 discount. Enclosed is my $25 for one year's worth of *Legacy*.

_____
name

_____
address

_____
city, state, zip

_____
area code and phone number

Dr. Gary North
Institute for Christian Economics
P.O. Box 8000
Tyler, TX 75711

Dear Dr. North:

I read about your organization in Ray Sutton's book, *Who Owns the Family?* I understand that you publish several newsletters that are sent out for six months free of charge. I would be interested in receiving them:

☐ *Biblical Economics Today*
  Christian Reconstruction
  and Dominion Strategies

Please send any other information you have concerning your program.

_____
name

_____
address

_____
city, state, zip

_____
area code and phone number

☐ Enclosed is a tax-deductible donation to help meet expenses.

Dominion Press • P.O. Box 8204 • Ft. Worth, TX 76124

The *Biblical Blueprints Series* is a multi-volume book series that gives Biblical solutions for the problems facing our culture today. Each book deals with a specific topic in a simple, easy to read style such as economics, government, law, crime and punishment, welfare and poverty, taxes, money and banking, politics, the environment, retirement, and much more.

Each book can be read in one evening and will give you the basic Biblical principles on each topic. Each book concludes with three chapters on how to apply the principles in your life, the church and the nation. Every chapter is summarized so that the entire book can be absorbed in just a few minutes.

As you read these books, you will discover hundreds of new ways to serve God. Each book will show you ways that you can start to implement God's plan in your own life. As hundreds of thousands join you, and millions more begin to follow the example set, a civilization can be changed.

Why will people change their lives? Because they will see God's blessings on those who live by His Word (Deuteronomy 4:6-8).

Each title in the *Biblical Blueprints Series* is available in a deluxe paperback edition for $6.95, or a classic leatherbound edition for $14.95.

The following titles are scheduled for publication in 1986:

- Introduction to Dominion: Biblical Blueprints on Dominion
- Honest Money: Biblical Blueprints on Money and Banking
- Who Owns the Family?: Biblical Blueprints on the Family and the State
- In the Shadow of Plenty: Biblical Blueprints on Welfare and Poverty
- Liberator of the Nations: Biblical Blueprints on Political Action
- Inherit the Earth: Biblical Blueprints on Economics
- Chariots of God: Biblical Blueprints on Defense
- The Children Trap: Biblical Blueprints on Education
- Entangling Alliances: Biblical Blueprints on Foreign Policy
- Ruler of the Nations: Biblical Blueprints on Government
- Protection of the Innocent: Biblical Blueprints on Crime and Punishment

Additional Volumes of the Biblical Blueprints Series are scheduled for 1987 and 1988.

Please send more information concerning this program.

_____
name

_____
address

_____
city, state, zip

Jesus said to "Occupy till I come." But if Christians don't control the territory, they can't occupy it. They get tossed out into cultural "outer darkness," which is just exactly what the secular humanists have done to Christians in the 20th century: in education, in the arts, in entertainment, in politics, and certainly in the mainline churches and seminaries. Today, the humanists are "occupying." But they won't be for long. *Backward, Christian Soldiers?* shows you why. This is must reading for all Christians as a supplement to the *Biblical Blueprints Series*. You can obtain a copy by sending $1.00 (a $5.95 value) to:

Institute for Christian Economics
P.O. Box 8000
Tyler, TX 75703

_____
name

_____
address

_____
city, state, zip

_____
area code and phone number